10.5

BRITISH ARTISTS
EDITED BY JOHN ROTHENSTEIN
DIRECTOR AND KEEPER
OF THE TATE GALLERY

PRE-RAPHAELITE PAINTERS
BY R. IRONSIDE & J. A. GERE

PHAIDON

JOHN EVERETT MILLAIS: THE RETURN OF THE DOVE TO THE ARK (Oil, 1850)

PRE-RAPHAELITE PAINTERS

BY ROBIN IRONSIDE

WITH A DESCRIPTIVE CATALOGUE

BY JOHN GERE

LONDON · THE PHAIDON PRESS LTD

1948

MADE IN GREAT BRITAIN

TEXT AND MONOCHROME PLATES PRINTED AT THE BAYNARD PRESS · LONDON

COLOUR PLATES PRINTED BY HENRY STONE & SONS LTD · BANBURY

FOREWORD

The author wishes to express his thanks to the various Museum authorities and private owners who have kindly given permission for works in their possession to be reproduced in this book. Special thanks for valuable assistance of various kinds in the preparation of the volume are due to Mr. C. F. Bell, Sir Sydney Cockerell, the late Mrs. Wykeham Deverell, Mrs. Leathart, Mr. Hugh Wyatt Standen, Sir Charles Trevelyan, Bt., Mrs. Maclaren Williams, and the staff of the Art Gallery, Johannesburg.

Grateful acknowledgments are also due to Mr. John Gere, the compiler of the Catalogue, by whose patience and energy the inclusion among the illustrations of several fine but little known pictures (some hitherto unpublished) was made possible. The selection of the plates has been made with the object of displaying the beauties of Pre-Raphaelite painting and not of presenting a historical survey of the movement's development.

LONDON 1948   R. I.

ALPHABETICAL LIST OF THE ARTISTS

CONTENTS

INTRODUCTION

THE birth of the Pre-Raphaelite movement was not an unheralded occasion, to be clearly dated from the conversations that took place in 1848 and 1849 between Holman Hunt, Millais and Rossetti, in which they endeavoured to define for themselves the inexpressible objects of their association, or from the appearance at the Academy in the latter year of Hunt's *Rienzi* and Millais' *Lorenzo and Isabella*.[1] The small but piercing voice then raised which still has, for many of us, such a singular attraction was one result only, one miniature crystallization of processes of thought and feeling that had long been operating in the minds of others, in the mind of Europe generally. Their operation can be traced from the productions of the Pre-Raphaelites' immediate elders to a relatively remote past. In 1844, William Dyce, who was pursuing, less tenaciously, the same path as that upon which the Pre-Raphaelites, with so much more urgency of purpose, set forth, had already begun his picture of *St. John leading Mary Magdalene from the Tomb*, a work which, when some years later it was finished, was characteristically Pre-Raphaelite— though it must fairly be admitted that the artist had then had sufficient opportunity of becoming aware of the tendentious beginnings of Millais and Holman Hunt, by whose practices he was in fact influenced. In the 1830's, John Frederick Lewis was elaborating in Cairo a water-colour style which, with its painful attention to the detailed rendering of accessories, its uncompromising accuracy of local colour, rivalled the most hair-splitting accomplishment of the young Millais. Doubtless, Lewis was strengthened in the course that he had, on his own account, adopted, by the justification it received, as it matured, from Pre-Raphaelitism, and from the praise of Ruskin, whose eloquence and patronage had made of Pre-Raphaelitism a fashionable, almost a popular thing. But, whatever the art of Dyce and Lewis may have received from the Brotherhood and its supporters, there was no such debt, no such sanction in the case of William Mulready's picture, *The Sonnet*, which was painted in 1836 and has much of the poetic sentiment and all the concise draughtsmanship of the work of Hunt, Millais and Rossetti in 1849; nor did Mulready, as Dyce certainly did, in any way succumb to the example of the Pre-Raphaelite style as it unfolded. The same may be said of the neglected art of Daniel Maclise, whose sculptural line, whose foliage that has been described as of malachite and whose predilection for chivalric themes foreshadowed the Pre-Raphaelite mode of expression and were venerated by Rossetti. Almost a generation earlier, in the first decade of the nineteenth century, German painters rebelled against international classicism and the more zealous among them joined together under the superintendence of Cornelius Overbeck in the brotherhood of the Nazarener, whose headquarters was established at a deserted monastery in the neighbourhood of Rome; these painters declared themselves, like the Pre-Raphaelites who came after them, as the votaries of Truth and Nature and openly emulated the happy innocence of style that they found to be a quality of the Italian painters before Raphael, an emulation which, however, unlike the corresponding ambitions of the English Pre-Raphaelites, was almost entirely Peruginesque in its results. In Germany itself, in the north, the Romantic vision of Philipp Otto Runge and Caspar David Friedrich had a clarity and exactness, if not a hardness, that might have given almost equal offence to the handful of critics, had they been called upon to judge it, who were so nettled, who felt themselves so challenged, by similar peculiarities in the maiden productions of Millais and Hunt. German painting of the period also exercised a direct influence upon the mould of Pre-Raphaelite style through the medium of Alfred Rethel's wood engravings, the first series of which appeared in 1847. The European sources of the style are more conspicuous in Germany than elsewhere; but elsewhere, also, even in the ranks of the extreme classicists, the broad propensities from which the Pre-Raphaelites struck their spark of beauty are discernible; we

---

[1] The Pre-Raphaelite Brotherhood was formed in 1848; the seven members were Rossetti, Holman Hunt, Millais, W. M. Rossetti (the artist's brother), F. G. Stephens, James Collinson and Thomas Woolner, the sculptor.

may recall the interest in the Quattrocento of Ingres and his disciples and the archaisms, somewhat earlier, of 'les Primitifs' and 'les Barbus' of the studio of David.

Such specific examples from the art of painting suffice, the more so because they are, to some extent, a random choice, to demonstrate that there was ample precedent for all the obvious insignia of the Pre-Raphaelite manner, for their mediævalism, for their rejection of what remained of eighteenth-century academism, for their love of careful detailed execution and even for their love of holding forth, through the vehicle of their art, on moral and religious issues, which had also tinctured the activities of the Nazarener, described by Goethe as Lenten preachers with the brush. These things, however, were not scattered, isolated phenomena; the artistic temper of the epoch vibrated with their presence, overt or hidden. Cultivated perception, at the beginning of the nineteenth century, was directed away from the general towards the particular; the very grasses and clouds came to be known by their particular species. The arts, furthermore, were interpenetrated by the historical sense; what might have justly been called neo-classic became, as archæology progressed, neo-Greek; in evoking the past, the imagination was increasingly tutored by research; and the majestic revival of the genius of Christianity with which the century opened provided artistic retrospection with a moral and religious focus in the Middle Ages, the ages of faith. Legitimacy and tradition, fleetingly linked with a spirit of scientific analysis, preponderated. Tennyson, *par excellence* the 'Pre-Raphaelite' poet, was the most illustrious English exponent of this pervading cultural pattern; there is almost an identity of sentiment and imagery between the poems of 1830 and the first productions of Pre-Raphaelitism. We may justly think of the Brotherhood as one expression of that phase of the Romantic Movement that was the flower of European reaction amid the ruins—predestined as they must then have seemed—of the ambitious generalizations of 1789.

Yet if, in considering the sources of the Pre-Raphaelite style, if, in seeking to assign to its brief, intense life the right place in the ravelled sequence of human inspiration, we can, without unduly straining the issue, point to related traits in the style of Ingres and his followers, then we need not feel deterred by logic from extending the comparison to David himself and, of course, to Flaxman; thence we may pursue the connection, on the one hand, backwards, via David, say, to Greuze, and thus, with apparent paradox, to the unlooked-for world of French rococo or, on the other hand, laterally, from Flaxman to Blake and the whole apparatus of the sublime and the horrific. It would require no particular ingenuity to prolong this process indefinitely and, provided there was the patience and discrimination to establish the myriad delicate links in the chain of indebtedness, the endless concatenation would be revealed as consequential and plausible. In art there is no sheer invention. There are modifications and developments; the faintest variation may be stressed in many and unforeseen ways, emphatically or insidiously, until the theme that had once suggested it seems, in retrospect, to betoken an alien principle, to have had no conceivable part in the fashioning of its own offspring; impelled by an intuitive recognition of purposes that lie implicit or unavowed in the achievements of the past, inspiration may speculate, take a sudden leap ahead, the intrepidity of which may have all the appearance of a break with history. But in fact the irresistible incitements of protean tradition are ceaselessly at work; an artist cannot but adhere, and adhere passionately, to the immortal example set by the genius of his predecessors. The true question to be considered by the critic is not that of the novelty of an artist's performance but, though the distinction may be a fine one, that of its speciality; a picture, it is evident, may be painted in the most conservative accordance with currently accepted canons and yet be a work of art of unique quality. Although the character of the Pre-Raphaelite movement did not take on, to any such extent, an accredited form, it was nevertheless of a much less startling kind than its earlier historians admitted ; nor, indeed, did it so perturb contemporary opinion as they were disposed to assume. At the same time, it emerged as, in the highest degree, a singular phenomenon.

The special attributes of the style were not developed by its authors over a protracted period of test and doubt, strewn with the failures of immaturity and full of the frustrations that beset a questing spirit; there was no experimental stage or half-way house. The main justificatory evidence

ARTHUR HUGHES: HOME FROM SEA (Oil, 1856-63)

for the movement had appeared before the painters concerned had reached the age of twenty-five. In a spasm of callow, youthful, nervous effort the whole of their importance (and, as we can now see, the whole of their ancestry) was brought to light. The vision was suddenly mature while the visionaries themselves were happily too immature to criticize its validity. The self-confident ardour that brought about or naturally attended this coincidence is one of the peculiarities of the movement. Out of it, but also out of the stylistic unanimity with which it was expressed, arose the force with which at the time the small explosion was felt. The concentrated power of the Brotherhood, in so far as it was more than an effect of the exuberance of youth, largely flowed from the hypnotic personality of Rossetti, who, in a quite extempore fashion, imposed upon its members the agonizing yoke of his young idealism, agonizing because submission required the cultivation at the same time of an inflamed imagination and a habit of fundamental brain work; Rossetti himself was liable to bite the carpet at painful moments when the combination seemed unlikely to be achieved. This tension of mind and spirit distinguished from other similar endeavours the Pre-Raphaelite determination to envisage the world sharply and clearly, to be delivered, rather late in the day as it may now appear, from the grumous tonal harmonies and trite rotundities of form that denaturalized the art of the 'history' painters quite as much as that of the popular, omnipresent purveyors of facetious genre, and even disfigured with a bedimming effect of complacent conformity, almost of punctilio, the works of painters so delightful as Stothard, Wilkie, Collins or Webster.

It was, at first, as if the Brotherhood looked at the world without eyelids; for them, a livelier emerald twinkled in the grass, a purer sapphire melted into the sea. On the illuminated page that nature seemed to thrust before their dilated pupils, every floating, prismatic ray, each drifting filament of vegetation, was rendered, in all its complexity, with heraldic brilliance and distinctness; the floor of the forest was carpeted not merely with the general variegation of light and shadow, but was seen to be plumed with ferns receiving each in a particular fashion the shafts of light that fell upon them; there were not simply birds in the branches above, but the mellow ouzel was perceived, fluting in the elm. As we read such a picture as Holman Hunt's *Hireling Shepherd*, in which the interest is ostensibly centred in the scene of seduction engaging the principal figures, our attention is repeatedly arrested, amid the general glare, by the vividly given intricacies of such minutiæ as the foreground weeds or the moth that spreads its wings across the shepherd's half-closed palm. Ford Madox Brown's *Work*, disregarding the majestic implications of its general intention, is a network of similar exquisitely fashioned clippings from the detail of life; and Millais' *Ophelia* expires amid a 'filtered tribute from the rough woodland' calculated to dazzle the spectator stamen by stamen. The Pre-Raphaelites transcribed nature analytically, 'selecting nothing and rejecting nothing,' and the labour that went into the copying of each particle was sharpened by a kind of frenzy which goaded them into a burnishing and polishing of their handiwork to a point beyond representation, at which it shone with a feverish clarity.

The vehement perseverance with which they worked was an extension of the force with which they felt their own conceptions. They were born into a romantic age, but also into an age of social constraint, one in which passion might hope, in life at least, for no richer reward than the fluttering of a handkerchief from some ivied casement. In respectable Victorian society man's emotional desires, in the absence of sufficient acknowledged outlet for their indiscriminate energies, reached a level of strange intensity. The narrow limits within which the movements of the heart were circumscribed by propriety, movements which, untrammelled, avail themselves of so wide a compass, produced an enhancing, rarefying effect; since vows were cruelly expected to be kept for ever, plighted love and the hesitant gestures that might easily in the circumstances induce it, the touch of a hand, or a blush perfectly if involuntarily timed, acquired a character of irrevocable sanctity. The broken pledge, in such a moral order, inflicted an incurable wound; the long engagement was a corroding interval of anxiety and frustration; and all April loves were tended and guarded in the fear that they might die before the harvesting. Life was brief, but love, it was believed, should be long, was, in its essential nature, long, potentially transcendental and everlasting. We might expect the most libidinous conception of society to associate with the vicissitudes of love a degree of ecstasy and anguish; it is not therefore surprising, when love's versatility is confined by convention, that its rewards, sparingly distributed, should appear to be of ineffable, even of divine worth and that the many who must be denied its sweetness should be reluctant to resign themselves to despair, preferring to envisage some compensation from their tragedy in the walks of paradise. The poetic temper of the time inclined to approximate divine to human love. The two were, for Coventry Patmore, who was engrossed by the sexual idea, almost identical; 'the relation of the soul to Christ,' he wrote, 'as his betrothed wife is a mine of undiscovered joy and power.' The most trivial incidents of romance as it might blossom in the highly unromantic scenery of contemporary middle class comfort struck him, as appears from the Angel in the House, as ennobled by the metaphysical symbolism he bestowed upon them. Simeon Solomon's Vision of Love gives expression to the same analogy but, as in Patmore's later poems, with a more grandiose imagery befitting the august nature of the affiliation. The poetry of the young Rossetti paid passionate tribute to the idea, and it is evident from the secular poems of his sister that her emotions were similarly attuned, though her adamantine adherence to orthodox Anglican belief held her will athirst against that light to the exclusion of more sensuous pieties. If orthodoxy could not accept the establishment, with its fleshly implications, of such a kinship, it was, mystically and imaginatively, widely held—still more widely hoped—that Love was as strong as Death. Dead lovers watched with longing eyes the door of heaven 'which opening, letting in, lets out no more'; their accents strove to be hearkened by those they had been parted from, who awaited, often in a state of faltering and distressed faith, the moment of reunion, the time when it would be sweet to die.

Faith faltered indeed; its abyss wore an ever more fearful aspect as scientific scepticism progressed, but the plunge into spiritual certainties, the assurance of celestial compensation remained a conceivably liberating resource for the maladjusted ones, of whom there must have been many in a world where practical ethics seemed to be increasingly at issue with ideas upon the origins and nature of man. Piety continued to be offered as a much vaunted solace to the bereaved and the oppressed, and also to the depraved. But just as belief in the eternal communion of souls was a bitter-sweet remedy for the sick of heart, so the efficacy of religion to relieve those who suffered more materially was not asserted without compunction. In the hungry forties, democratic positivism agitated the sphere of political action, and its warming influence was felt by all sensitive minds, however abstracted they might be, in some palace of art, from the household woes of the period; where labour seemed to have lost its dignity, the loss was seen to be attributable as much to the state of society as to the baseness of the labourer; there was an artistic contemplation of economic misery that was not only compassionate, but also saint-simonien. Ruskin's radicalism trailed in its wake no artist such as Courbet; for fleeting moments, however, the spirit of Courbet was manifest in English art—telepathically manifest, for there was no conscious, nor at first glance is there any apparent, relation; there was simply, and quite ephemerally, the same attack upon reality, the same affectionate pity for it. It was the attitude of Crabbe rather than of Wordsworth that prevailed. The murmurs of those who toiled in the murk, tied to desk, counter or machine, were the murmurs not of sinners, but of poor slaves imploring peace. The nuptial carriage of the poor began to wear the aspect of a 'hearse, blighted with plagues'; and, it was noticed, children were sold by their fathers while yet their tongues could scarcely utter. But this realistic, sceptical attitude and the germ of philanthropic indignation that grew together with it, were simply an omen impotent, for the time being, against the established economic order—more impotent than against mere moral durance—powerful, only, to sow a seed of painful doubt in the minds of many who continued to uphold the social and material inequalities that were in force. There existed a state of uncertain or hardly won faith in the existence of heaven and a swerving conviction that on earth the fittest might be expected to survive.

Such were distinctive features of the moral and imaginative atmosphere which the Pre-Raphaelites absorbed and which they exhaled in acrid breaths through the rather softening filter of their art. We are at once aware, in looking at their pictures, of an anguish held in reserve, of a suspicion, almost a wish, that the foundations of life, as they were generally known, might instantly dissolve under sufficient pressure. Despite the moral warning that it utters, there is a note of lyrical wickedness in Holman Hunt's *Hireling Shepherd*, of almost delighted awe in his *Awakened Conscience*. The Ariel that lures Millais' *Ferdinand* has a demoniac appearance that seems to predict allurements beyond the limits of any ordinary Fairyland. The aggravation, that nearly amounted to etiquette, of the torments and assuagements of romantic love, its foam and fret, is reflected in such works as Millais' drawing *Accepted* with the happy suitor's gesture of cathartic prostration; it is acknowledged in Windus' *Burd Helen*, who, like Käthchen von Heilbronn, follows her chosen but indifferent master barefoot on whatever thorny path he may pursue. The unmitigable finality of chance interruptions to the course of true love is displayed in the same painter's *Too Late*, a story of the shattering of two lives by the depredations of phthisis in one of them. How difficult it was to be unashamedly demonstrative, and for how much poetry and desire, therefore, the smallest sign might count, is perceptible as the unacknowledged theme of many of the most acutely felt Pre-Raphaelite paintings. Arthur Hughes' *The Tryst* seems to represent, physically, no more than a confrontation. Emotionally, however, the meeting is full of mutual passion and mutual doubt that acquire a spiritual vehemence from their repression, and do not overflow into action, because they are held in check tightly, if not quite securely, by what can now be called cynical standards of behaviour; were this restrictive thread to snap, we may feel, the pair might touch and devour one another; there is a cankerous beauty in the green meadow of their tryst. It is the same constriction that inspires Millais' *Waiting* and is the whole agonizing burthen of *The Long Engagement* by Arthur Hughes. It was a constriction that could be borne because the penalties of liberation were so grievous or because, for bold and ardent natures, endurance was the guarantee of spiritual rewards—though reliance on such rewards had the effect of increasing the stringency of earthly relations; the widow who in Millais' *Ghost* unthinkingly betrothes herself a second time is stayed at the altar by the spectre of her first love. Millais has also given us a sharp picture of the material penalty that might follow transgression in a less uncommon field of experience in his drawing, *Retribution*, which tells of the fateful intrusion upon a husband and his innocent young wife of a discarded woman entreating support for her children. Such tragedies were not only made unjustifiably likely but also unjustifiably dire by the rigid structure of social life; the pathetic necessity

FIG. I. JOHN EVERETT MILLAIS : THE GHOST. PEN AND INK, C. 1853

whereby moral delinquency was deemed to be succeeded by utter ruin is affectingly expressed in Rossetti's unfinished *Found*, in which 'Love deflowered and sorrow of none avail' meet by chance in the persons of a young farm hand driving a calf to market, the symbolic sacrifice, as it might be, of some helpless boyish passion, and a girl once his promised wife, but now a creature confessedly degraded beyond recovery.

It must be admitted that in *Found* there is no positive expression of indignation at the circumstances that might induce such irremediable collapse; indeed, it is probable that Rossetti, who was fond of chance encounters, would, had he picked up the girl himself, have regarded her condition as neither irremediable nor even, possibly, as a collapse. But the Pre-Raphaelite movement was certainly excited by a disturbed inkling of the social injustices around them. Ford Madox Brown's *Work*, even more in its way an *allégorie du réel* than Courbet's *Atelier*, is a clear reformist gesture, and, in so far as it offers for inspection and, at the same time, pronounces upon, the daily realities of the period, it is comparable with Courbet's *Casseurs de Pierres* or *Cribleuses de Blé*. None of the original Pre-Raphaelites could have adopted Courbet's extreme plebeian posture, but Brown acknowledged 'twinges' of socialism, twinges which, in *Work*, he does not scruple to convey through the images of his group of motherless children abandoned by a drunken father and in a state of 'extreme dilapidation,' of his hump-backed beer-vendor who, as a child, 'was probably starved, stunted with gin and suffered to get run over,' and of his policeman who wilfully upsets the fragile wares of an orange-girl. A forcible expression (despite the proliferation of these significant details) of unpenetrating fellow-feeling with Labour greets us at first glance of this picture in the angular, rock-like, threatening nucleus of British workmen round which the less confident symbols, including a representation of the unheeding rich, circle rather obscurely. Sympathy, strongly mixed with horror and fascination, described the limit of Pre-Raphaelite positivism, but it was a limit strained by what it embraced. We perceive the discomfort of the tension in Millais' *Virtue and Vice*, in which a poverty-stricken seamstress is represented as having no support beyond the cold fact of her respectability and the inadequate earnings of her needle, and in the vagrant child of his *Race Meeting*, who lurks beneath the carriage wheels of the wealthy, an undiscerning spectator of their profligacy and ruin.

In giving way, as they could not help giving way to the pressure of this sympathy, the Pre-Raphaelites found themselves on the fringe of questions which, driven to their revolutionary issue, might have borne the less purely artistic investigator, as they bore Ruskin and Morris, away from the charmed enclave in which bitterness and the soul's hunger could be exorcized through imagery, into an area of pamphlets, public demonstrations and police courts where art, perhaps, would have withered or been forsaken. An instinct withheld them, quivering, on the brink of this possible transition, but, almost simultaneously they turned, and made their protest in a manner permitting their imagination to expand rather than subjecting it to a harrowing if not chilling concentration upon the cramped actuality of the times. The literature and history of the Middle Ages provided them with a less exacting outlet for the perturbation of their emotions, less exacting not because the tension was relaxed in contemplation of the polychromatic trappings of the world of Dante, Chaucer and Jacques de Voragines, but because it was a world which, though its permutations in the mind were illimitable, was immune from the encroachments of the social question. The tension of the heart strings in this recreated atmosphere was as high as ever and was suffered with finer excuse; the transcendental view of the affections was more decorously related to the age of chivalry than to the age of propriety; where love was raised upon a dais of silk, embroidered with fleur-de-lys and carved in doves and pomegranates, where it moved in chambers hung with arras, rose, amber, emerald and blue, its sanctity was less problematic, its magniloquent litanies were more fervently declaimed and its strict table of laws seemed easier to acknowledge. It might even, fair, delicate, of irresolute mien, inaptly personify itself (with eyes soft or falcon-clear?) to strengthen believers by the touch of its wing feathers or some other perceptible sign not less strengthening, if it was one that pierced instead of caressing. In its service, frail ships, adorned with rows of painted shields, crossed difficult seas; through its agency, flowers had been known to spring up through the tiled floors of turret rooms as symbolic proof that death is only the shadow of life and that love is simply more brilliantly there when life and the shadow it cast are gone. There was no material degradation awaiting transgressors in this artificial kingdom; the bitterness of Launcelot's disgrace at last overflowed in an apple orchard, to the sound of a distant bell. Sentence of eternal fire had a majesty, however appalling, and there was less temptation to incur it where everything conspired to make conformity in the court of love always a gracious, whether also a forlorn or despairing, duty. It is as subject to such an ornamented moral environment that Holman Hunt's Ferdinand and Isabella confer together, that Millais' Ophelia, more exalted than mad, floats into eternity and that Rossetti's Virgin Mary sits with her books, her seven-thorned briar and seven-leaved palm, emblems of her pre-election; religion and romance were more than ever entwined in this quattrocento world that the Pre-Raphaelites re-fashioned in their own image.

Rossetti was both the herald and the master in this imaginative recoil from the contemporary prospect. After the initial exhausting effort that had brought forth the two oil paintings *The Girlhood of Mary Virgin* and *Ecce Ancilla Domini*, exhausting because the artist had no natural technical proficiency, he began to seek relief from the sentiments which consumed him through the less professionalized, less methodical and more enigmatic medium of water-colour, and it is in the burning succession of small water-colours painted during the fifties and early sixties of the century that the mediævalism of the movement was most persuasively expressed. To the Anglo-Italian, Dante and Beatrice were an ever-present apparition; they came to him providing the highest sanction for and, indeed, inspiring, offering a finished vessel for all the intuitive refinements of his strong natural feelings. They came apparelled in garments of deep colour, and trailing illogically in their wake the brittle splendours of fifteenth-century illumination. In tessellations, bright, dry powderings of paint, meticulously disposed, as, it might be, for the mixing of some dangerous elixir, Rossetti set down his peculiar conception of these glories, of a *Vita Nuova*, not to be realized in space, but filling the recesses of the mind, a life to which strict canalization of the passions was befitting. *Dante's Dream*, *Dante's Vision of Rachel and Leah*, *Dante Drawing an Angel* and, most potent of all, *Arthur's Tomb* and *The Wedding of St. George*—poetic moments, compressed, condensed on to the paper—show with what curious force the artist's emotions could work within the compass of trellised arbours or pointed alcoves, narrow settings reminiscent not of Dante but of such *enlumineurs* as the author of *L'Histoire d'un Cœur d'Amour Epris*. For Rossetti, Elizabeth Siddall played the part of Beatrice or of the Damsel of the Holy Grail or other frail, ideal presence from mediæval literature. His love for her, it must be admitted, was impaired by spells of fanciful indifference, even by excursions with others who provided necessary though ephemeral satisfactions. But what true love, it may be asked, provides any satisfactions at all and, in posing such a question, must not sympathy go out to those who delude themselves with a faith in the perpetuation beyond the grave of erotic ties—spiritual in their essence as such loyalties may appear to be? Rossetti's devotion, however wavering its course, was both true and profound. The price which he attached, in common with other idealists of the time, to romantic desire, was such that even when, as in his case, there were no obstacles to its earthly fulfilment, it still seemed to require the crowning attribute of supernatural duration. The mystic, the tragic, element in his affection was proof against the sobering effects of complete reciprocation; so deeply indeed was this element interfused that the conjugal tie, though it was in fact contracted, set an obtrusive seal upon a relationship that claimed a more nebulous sanction. In spite of the quotidian obligations of marriage, in spite of the impossibility of producing, palpably, the exquisite conditions that would have helped so decisively to purify the flame of his attachment, Rossetti succeeded, with more picturesque success than any other contemporaneous lover, in casting, so to speak, a perceptible aureole about the object of his adoration and in endowing his feelings for her with a manifest poetry that protested victoriously against the unpromising background of the age. Under the spell of his attentions, Elizabeth Siddall became the muse of the Brotherhood; her earthly passage, sad and mysterious, was untimely completed; but her inspiration lingered and, for a moment, in Rossetti's breast, even recruited strength, enabling him to paint a posthumous revelation of her as Beatrice, wrapped in a deeply lit, nether-worldly, medicated atmosphere, a revelation which surpassed, in its dim splendour and the devoutness of its feeling, any previous metamorphosis she had incurred through the medium of his art.

The measure of emotional security which the Pre-Raphaelites may have obtained by directing increasingly their creative vision upon the poetry and symbolism of a chivalrous and graceful past did not at first in any way weaken the dissident character of their works. As, in their subjects from contemporary life, they did not refrain from portraying its ugliness and its dangers and thus implicitly criticized its structure, so, in fancifully re-interpreting the themes of mediæval romance and religion, they projected a world in which the pursuit of strict ideals was favoured by the beauty of every attendant circumstance, a support with which they were entirely unprovided in the existence they actually endured. In all its aspects, their art was a protest against this existence; nothing could be more mistaken than to regard them as Victorian. Art in the nineteenth century adopted, or was driven to adopt, the nonconformist position in which it is still entrenched; a majority of the great names, in literature and the arts, of the Victorian era were of those who raised their voices against it or whose utterance was obscure to the generation in which they lived. An essential element, however ineffective we may find it to be, in the quality of Pre-Raphaelite painting is to be sought in the emphasis with which it discountenanced the unsightliness of the times. The admiring amusement which is, possibly, the whole substance of the lingering popularity of Victoriana, and which appears, also, to be an ingredient of the present interest in the Pre-Raphaelites and their endeavours, is, when the latter are its object, the affectation of ignorance and insensibility. To confound the appreciation of Landseer and Winterhalter with that, for example, of such shrill expressions of feeling as Windus' *Too Late* or Brown's *Last of England*, is to mismatch what is fundamental in the first with what is irrelevant in the second; whatever Victorian elegancies may adorn the paintings of the Pre-Raphaelites, theirs was an uneasy spirit which, had it not failed to applaud the authentic æsthetic graces of the contemporary drawing-room, at least would have judged them too isolated to exert any brightening influence upon the encircling gloom. When the Pre-Raphaelites fail, their mistakes are grotesque, but no more amusing than their successes; bad Pre-Raphaelite art tends to be the outcome of over-emphatic expression, of vulgar licence injudiciously granted to questionable levels of passion and piety, the exposure of which is painful rather than entertaining to the sensitive spectator. It is difficult to contemplate without real discomfiture such works—to quote two striking examples—as Holman Hunt's *Shadow of the Cross* or Millais' *Prescribed Royalist*. Comment upon these shortcomings, which discretion might otherwise leave unnoticed, is made in this instance with pardonable uncharitableness since the same disturbed stream of feeling is an impulse behind the Pre-Raphaelite's richest achievements. These, whatever the mutations of taste, will always preserve the character of national treasures; their laborious finish, the dædalian elaboration, borne more frequently of nervous determination than of natural aptitude, with which their smallest parts were brought to completion, gives them a quality of rarity and 'virtu', that is much less open to dispute than their quality as works of art. But today, when much of what is best in painting is of an intimately expressionistic kind, we may well insist on the value of Pre-Raphaelite art as the effective æsthetic vehicle of private passion, as the distinct revelation of an inner disturbance and enthusiasm both in its themes and in the disquieting manner of their execution, the awkward constraint of gesture and attitude in the treatment of the figure, the feverish precision of drawing and occasional almost toxic virulence of colour.

Pitiably as it may now seem, and perhaps fatefully, the agitated creative spirit which in the beginning seemed to fuse the emotions of the Brotherhood was rapidly extinguished; it may have been too intense to be sustained for long and too weak to resist the pressure of the society it sought to enlighten —a weakness which might have changed into resilience had the pressure been less diluted by a corrupting admixture of favour and patronage that exacted concessions rather than tested resistance. By 1863 the inspiration that had been kindled in 1849 had perished. The Brotherhood was already dissolving in 1853, and as the decade came to an end, genuine manifestations of its somewhat infirm genius grew infrequent and spasmodic. Claimed by the demands of an expanding market for the mere productions of his technical brilliance, Millais renounced the less rewarding enthusiasms of his youth; *Autumn Leaves*, painted in 1856, is the last of his pictures in which the arduousness of poetic feeling is clearly revealed. Holman Hunt had, by 1858, relapsed into a laboured, sometimes an unsavoury, religiosity, which was conveyed without any of the controlled poignancy with which the *Hireling Shepherd* is penetrated and which is still effective in *The Scapegoat* of 1854. Rossetti's posthumous portrait of his wife, *Beata Beatrix*, painted in 1863, is the fitting term of his main artistic achievement; but, as more amply conceived and more academically carried out than his earlier work, it is also the presage of the ensuing series of repetitive female likenesses taken from a narrow range of favoured models, whose massive type was described by a French critic as '*apte à lancer les rudes balles de bois dans les links*,' but who represented for the artist—sometimes, perhaps, sardonically since his representations of them fetched rising prices—such legendary conceptions as Astarte, Venus or the Bride of the Song of Solomon. Delicate and imaginative as are the accoutrements of these sitters in their various roles, their large and enigmatic features, 'enthroned', to use Rossetti's phraseology, upon 'a round, reared neck, meet column of Love's shrine', seem to be prurient without adequately symbolizing the heights of romance or depths of voluptuousness in the characters assigned to them. These later paintings have nothing of the complex and affecting structure of the best passages from the *House of Life*, with which, to an uncertain extent, they are contemporaneous. They record the decline of the painter, a decline which was artificially promoted by the ingloriousness of pandering though, unlike Millais, Rossetti was largely the creator of the taste which, for his ultimate reputation, he so unwarily supplied. The zeal of the less conspicuous painter members of the Brotherhood was not more lasting. But, although its transience may be ascribed to original lack of faculty or inclination, in the case of James Collinson and Frederick Stephens, whose adherence was secured chiefly in order to raise the membership to seven, both artists were sensibly infected by the inspiration of the moment and produced vividly Pre-Raphaelite works before resigning an affiliation to whose exaction their talents were unequal. Those artists who, by the stress of their sensibilities, were impelled within the Pre-Raphaelite orbit were quite as subject to the evanescence of the contagion as those whose collaboration was less spontaneously given. The art of Arthur Hughes, who, under the spell of Millais and Rossetti, had painted as intensely and sometimes with a more insinuating sweetness than either, failed to survive the decadence of his models. Madox Brown, whose youthful connection with the Nazarener had stamped his art with a character to which the Pre-Raphaelites appealed as determining their own, was, in his turn, fired by the precarious unity of his disciples, but only, in due course, to recidivate into a more or less fluent style of historical painting which dispensed with the perfectionist standards of Pre-Raphaelite technique. The inwrought spirit of the Brotherhood was a momentary irradiation; but its light was everywhere felt, and, as it began to fade, confused without illuminating a small crowd of vain, sometimes unknowing or unwilling proselytes—such unequal painters as Frederick Sandys, Noel Paton or William Bell Scott—whose art was distinguished by the frequency of mediævalistic adornments or by a distressing unction of sentiment immune from the prophylactic anxiety that had exalted the moralities of 'primitive' Pre-Raphaelitism.

The original impulses were consumed by those who had felt them, but, in one sense, the direction they indicated was fruitfully modified and the art of Burne-Jones may be represented as the gracious and lingering twilight of an ephemeral heyday. He was attracted, with William Morris, to the Pre-Raphaelites by their fanciful and sanguine view of the beauty and felicity of past epochs. His first paintings were faithful echoes of Rossetti's evocations of Romance; Morris accompanied him so far, but enflamed by the desire to improve by practical measures the protest inherent in Pre-Raphaelitism he most usefully diverted his energy to the applied arts and eventually to politics. The gifts of Burne-Jones, of a much more delicate nature, lacked vehemence even to sustain the denunciatory note in painting. The unsubstantial region that he created out of legendary history provided a retreat rather than a romantic contrast; his art seems to solicit its admirers to cultivate their dreams and allow the grass of the earth to grow weeds under their feet. Amid the company of his goddesses and princesses, motionless or loitering, in dresses of indefinable hue that swept from their sides like water flowing away, the fire that had animated Rossetti's youth was gently and finally quenched. Imperceptibly 'there was ice with the warm blood mixing'; the 'sallow-rifted glooms of evening' softly covered the brightness of the Brotherhood's original vision. But this emphasis on the independent value of the day-dream had its own validity; the want of beautiful conditions of living, that was implicitly expressed by the Pre-Raphaelite movement and which Morris endeavoured unremittingly to supply, may be one that can never be appeased. Efforts to obtain the unobtainable are, possibly, their own reward and sometimes leave an indelible impress behind them; there are, however, refinements of life to be derived from the studied exploitation of fantasies that can only be termed vain when their melancholy beauty is defiled by hopes of their factual accomplishment; such refinements it was Burne-Jones' fitful talent to communicate. Through his more successful pictures, *Green Summer*, for example, or the *Perseus* series, we are initiated into a grave, ceremonious, miraculous world in which the fiercest conflicts resolve themselves into a solemn mime and passion is continually relieved by wishful meditations in enchanted groves. Abroad, imaginative painting of this character proved a fertile seed; Puvis de Chavanne's limpid narrations of a Saturnian age had an inspiring effect upon the magnificent and influential art of Gauguin. In this country, the aspirations of youth were diverted by the unseasonable but lively eruption of English Impressionism. The conceptions of Burne-Jones were frequently and feebly imitated. Only Beardsley, for a moment, delicately distended their limits; the 'æstheticism' to which he subscribed, more prominent in literature than in art, may be regarded as a last direct mutation of Pre-Raphaelite influence. But it is certain that English romantic painting will be recurringly compelled, if not predisposed, to reckon with the rare, narrow summits to which Pre-Raphaelitism was laboriously lifted in the virgin agitation of its spirits.

LONDON 1946   ROBIN IRONSIDE

FIG. 2. FORD MADOX BROWN : AN ENGLISH AUTUMN AFTERNOON. OIL, 1852-4.

CATALOGUE

CATALOGUE

The artists are arranged in a roughly chronological order according to the year of their birth

WILLIAM BELL SCOTT

1811 Edinburgh—1890 Penkill, Ayrshire

IRON AND COAL, canvas, 74 × 74.   PLATES 1-3
Coll. Sir Charles Trevelyan, Bt.

The son of an engraver, and younger brother of David Scott (1806-49), one of the most interesting, and undeservedly forgotten, nineteenth-century romantic painters, William Bell Scott was an early friend of Rossetti, and contributed to *The Germ* in 1850. He held, however, a post in the Government School of Design in Newcastle from 1844 to 1864, and this prevented him from playing any considerable part in the Pre-Raphaelite Movement, as he would almost certainly have done if he had been in London during those years. His closest association with Rossetti was from 1864 to 1882, when they were neighbours in Chelsea.

Scott was also a poet, and a prolific critical writer on subjects connected with literature and art. He wrote a memoir of his brother, and was one of the first people in this country to call attention to the early German schools of painting.

His curiously frustrated, crotchety personality (most clearly revealed in his 'Autobiographical Notes') is perhaps more interesting to us to-day than his actual pictures or poems.

Iron and Coal is part of a decorative scheme, instigated at Wallington Hall by Pauline, Lady Trevelyan, the friend of Swinburne and Ruskin, for the large central courtyard of the house, which had been roofed over and made into a hall: it is the last of a series of eight large paintings illustrating the history of Northumberland from Roman times, and must be one of the very first representations of heavy industry in art. It clearly owes much to Madox Brown's *Work* (q.v. Plate 8), in, for instance, such details as the little girl in the foreground; but Scott's point of view is entirely detached, and *Iron and Steel* has none of the ethical implications of *Work*.

WILLIAM DYCE

1806 Aberdeen—1864 Streatham

Of an earlier generation than the true Pre-Raphaelites, as a young student in Rome during the 1820's, Dyce came into contact with the German 'Nazarene' group. He became a successful portrait painter in Edinburgh during the next decade, and in the 1840's was one of the pioneers in the revival of fresco painting. On the death of Shee he was offered, but declined, the Presidency of the Royal Academy.

PEGWELL BAY, canvas, 24½ × 34½.   PLATE 4
National Gallery, London.
Exh. R.A. 1860.

Begun in 1858: the comet of that year appears in the sky. 'Verily the very name of the place brings with it a savour of shrimp sauce ; and it is here storied in a picture of heartbreaking elaboration.' (*The Art Journal*, 1860.)

GEORGE HERBERT AT BEMERTON, canvas, 33 × 44. PLATE 5
Guildhall Art Gallery, London.
Exh. R.A. 1861.

George Herbert (1593-1633), the poet and Anglican divine, was Vicar of Bemerton, a village near Salisbury. The spire of Salisbury Cathedral can be seen in the background.

AUGUSTUS LEOPOLD EGG

1816 London—1863 Algiers

Egg made his name, like his friend and contemporary Frith, with scenes from literature and history in the literary romantic style of Leslie and Newton. In taste and generosity, however, he was in advance of his colleagues in the Academy, for in 1849 he introduced himself to Holman Hunt to congratulate him on *Rienzi*, and remained a champion of the Pre-Raphaelites and a loyal friend, particularly to Holman Hunt. Pre-Raphaelite influence, diluted, is apparent in his work of the late 1850's; *Past and Present* (Tate Gallery) owes something to Hunt's *Awakening Conscience* as well as to Frith, but Ruskin laid his finger on the essential difference between Egg and the Pre-Raphaelites when he wrote, of *Cromwell*, '. . . hardly strange enough to have the look of reality . . . a picture which is not at first a little wonderful to us, can hardly at last be true to us.'

CROMWELL BEFORE NASEBY, canvas, 40 × 50.   PLATE 6
Royal Academy Diploma Gallery, Burlington House.
Exh. R.A. 1859.

FORD MADOX BROWN

1821 Calais—1893 London

Madox Brown's development can be divided into three distinct periods. From 1837 to 1846 he was studying on the Continent: in Antwerp under Baron Wappers, in Paris, and in Rome, where he met Cornelius and Overbeck, the surviving members of the German 'Nazarene' or 'Pre-Raphaelite' group; the earlier works of this period, such as *The Execution of Mary Queen of Scots*, are in the international romantic style, but in later pictures, such as *Wickliffe reading the Bible to John of Gaunt* and *Chaucer in the House of Edward III*, Nazarene influence can be seen. In 1848 Rossetti introduced himself, and asked Brown to take him as a pupil. This arrangement did not last long, but he and Rossetti remained close friends. He was not asked to join the P.R.B., but from 1849 to *c.* 1863 or 1864, Brown's works may be called entirely Pre-Raphaelite. His later pictures, which are influenced more specifically by Rossetti, increased, not altogether to their advantage, in sensuous and romantic qualities.

WORK, canvas, $53 \times 77\frac{1}{8}$, signed and dated *F. Madox Brown 1852-65.*   PLATES 7-10
Manchester City Art Gallery.

Begun in 1852. Painted about half-way up Heath Street, Hampstead, on the west side, looking up the hill; most details of the background can still be recognized. Rossetti spoke of it as illustrating 'all kinds of Carlylianisms', and that this was the artist's deliberate intention is made clear by the introduction of portraits of Carlyle and the Rev. F. D. Maurice, a leader of the Christian Socialist Movement. In a long explanation of the picture, printed in full on pp. 189-95 of Hueffer's *Life*, which helps one to appreciate Rossetti's remark to Hall Caine that Brown was 'as sententious as Dr. Johnson', he declared that the theme was '*Work* as it now exists, with the British excavator for a central group, as the outward and visible type of *Work*.' Round these he placed other figures: on the bank under the trees, men for various reasons unemployed; the beggar with his tray of flowers; a group of motherless children in mourning, under the care of their elder sister; the brain-workers, Carlyle and Maurice, who 'seeming to be idle, work, and are the cause of well-ordained work in others', a hunchback with a beer-tray, who typifies 'town pluck and energy contrasted with country thews and sinews'; and the rich, typified by two ladies, the younger (a portrait of the artist's wife), whose 'only business in life is to dress and look beautiful for our benefit', and the elder, who 'devotes her energies to tract-distributing', also by a gentleman (a portrait of R. B. Martineau) and his daughter on horseback.

Detail of WORK.   PLATE 8
'Bobus, our old friend, "the sausage-maker of Houndsditch" from *Past and Present*, having secured a colossal fortune (he boasts of it *now*), by anticipating the French Hippophage Society in the introduction of horse-flesh as a *cheap* article of human food, is at present going in for the county of Middlesex, and, true to his old tactics, has hired all the idlers in the neighbourhood to carry his boards. These being one too many for the bearers, an old woman has volunteered to carry the one in excess.'

Detail of WORK.   PLATE 9
Heads of Carlyle and Frederick Denison Maurice; ' The Brain-Workers.'

Detail of WORK.   PLATE 10
'The ragged wretch who has never been *taught* to *work*, with his restless gleaming eyes he doubts and despairs of everyone. But for a certain effeminate gentleness of disposition and a love of nature, he might have been a burglar! He lives in Flower and Dean Street, where the policemen walk two and two, and the worst cut-throats surround him, but he is harmless; and before the dawn you may see him miles out in the country, collecting his wild weeds and singular plants to awaken interest, and perhaps find a purchaser in some sprouting botanist.' The posters behind the head of this man have on them the names of 'The Working Men's College', founded in 1854 by F. D. Maurice, where Brown taught drawing for many years, and of the 'Boys' Home, 41 Euston Road', an enterprise in which Brown's patron, the collector, Colonel Gillum, was much interested.

Brown's sonnet on *Work* is dated 1865.

'Work, which beads the brow and tans the flesh
Of lusty manhood, casting out its devils.
By whose weird art transmuting poor men's evils,
Their bed seems down, their one dish ever fresh.
Ah me. For lack of it what ills in leash
Holds us. 'Tis want the poor mechanic levels
To workhouse depths, while Master Spendthrift revels
For want of work, the fiends him soon enmesh.

Ah, beauteous tripping dame with bell-like skirts,
Intent on thy small scarlet coated hound,
Are ragged wayside babes not lovesome too?
Untrained, their state reflects on thy deserts,
Or they grow noisome beggars to abound,
Or dreaded midnight robbers breaking through.'

'TAKE YOUR SON, SIR!', canvas, $27\frac{1}{2} \times 15$, signed and insc. *F. M. Brown, Take your son sir.*   PLATE 11
Tate Gallery, London.

Begun in 1851, being a portrait of the artist's wife: resumed in 1857 after the canvas had been enlarged, but never finished.

'THE PRETTY BAA-LAMBS' (sometimes called *Summer's Heat*), canvas, $23\frac{1}{2} \times 29\frac{1}{2}$, signed and dated *F. Madox Brown 1851-9.*   PLATE 12
Brown's first *plein-air* landscape, begun at Stockwell in 1851. He records in his diary: 'The Baa-Lamb picture was painted almost entirely in sunlight, which twice gave me a fever while painting. . . . my painting room being on a level with the garden, Emma [his wife] sat for the lady and Kate [his daughter] for the child. The lambs and sheep used to be brought from Clapham Common in a truck: one of them ate up all the flowers one morning in the garden, where they used to behave very ill. The background was painted on the common.'
A smaller, and much less detailed version, made in 1853 (Ashmolean Museum, Oxford), is well known. I have not so far been able to trace the whereabouts of the original, reproduced here. It was in the Leathart Collection until 1896, and was exhibited in that year at the Goupil Gallery with the rest of the collection. It must have been sold from this exhibition, for it was not in the subsequent sale at Christie's.
'This picture was painted in 1851, and exhibited the following year, at a time when discussion was very rife on certain ideas and principles in art, very much in harmony with my own views, but more sedulously promulgated by friends of mine. Hung in a false light, and viewed through the medium of false ideas, the painting was, I think, much misunderstood. I was told that it was impossible to make out what *meaning* I had in the picture. At the present moment, few people, I trust, will seek for any meaning beyond the obvious one, that is—a lady, a baby, two lambs, a servant maid, and some grass. In all cases, pictures must be judged first as pictures—a deep philosophical intention will not make a fine picture, such being rather given in excess of the bargain; and though all epic works of art have this excess, yet I should be much inclined to doubt the genuineness of that artist's ideas who never painted from love of the mere look of things, whose mind was always on the stretch for a moral. This picture was painted out in the sunlight; the only intention being to render that effect as well as my powers in a first attempt of that kind would allow.' (F. M. Brown, 1865, Exh. Cat.)

THE TRAVELLER, watercolour and body colour, $12 \times 18\frac{3}{4}$.
Signed and dated, *FMB '68.*   PLATE 13
Fitzwilliam Museum, Cambridge.

Hueffer states that this drawing illustrated a poem by Victor Hugo, about a 'traveller riding through a village at nightfall, when all the world beside is resting.' The subject was engraved on wood and published in *Once a Week* for February, 1869; according to Hueffer, to accompany a translation of the poem by Brown himself. No such translation, however, seems to have appeared.

AN ENGLISH AUTUMN AFTERNOON, canvas, oval, $27\frac{1}{2} \times 53$.
Signed *F. Madox Brown.*   FIG. 2 and PLATE 14
Birmingham Art Gallery.

THE LAST OF ENGLAND, panel, almost circular, $32\frac{1}{2} \times 29\frac{1}{2}$, signed and dated *F. Madox Brown 1855.*   PLATE 15
Birmingham Art Gallery.

In 1852, at the height of the Gold Rush, Woolner left for the Australian goldfields to seek his fortune; Brown, also depressed by failure and poverty, and seriously considering the idea of emigrating to India, saw him off at Gravesend. This picture, depicting himself and his wife as emigrants, was the result; he was engaged on it from 1852 to 1855.

He later wrote of it: 'This picture is, in the strictest sense, historical. It treats of the great Emigration Movement which attained its culminating point in 1865. . . . I have, in order to present the parting scene in its fullest tragic development, singled out a couple from the middle classes, high enough through education and refinement to appreciate all that they are now giving up. . . . The husband broods bitterly over blighted hopes and severance from all that he has been striving for. . . . To insure the peculiar look of *light all round* which objects have on a dull day at sea, it was painted for the most part in the open air on dull days, and, when the flesh was being painted, on cold days. Absolutely without regard to the art of any period or country, I have tried to render this scene as it would appear. The minuteness of detail which would be visible under such conditions of broad daylight I have thought necessary to imitate as bringing the pathos of the subject home to the beholder.[1]
He also wrote a sonnet on the subject, dated 1865.

> ' "The last of England! O'er the sea, my dear,
>   Our homes to seek amid Australian fields.
>   Us, not our million-acred island yields
>   The space to dwell in. Thrust out. Forced to hear
>   Low ribaldry from sots, and share rough cheer
>   From rudely nurtured men. The hope youth builds
>   Of fair renown, bartered for that which shields
>   Only the back, and half-formed lands that rear
>
>   The dust-storm blistering up the grasses wild.
>   There learning skills not, nor the poets dream,
>   Nor aught so loved as children shall we see."
>   She grips his listless hand and clasps her child;
>   Through rainbow tears she sees a sunnier gleam.
>   She cannot see a void, where he will be.'

WALTON-ON-THE-NAZE, canvas, $12\frac{1}{2} \times 16\frac{1}{2}$.   PLATE 16
Birmingham Art Gallery.
Begun in the autumn of 1859, finished the next year.

CARRYING CORN, canvas, $7\frac{1}{2} \times 10\frac{1}{2}$, signed and dated *F. Madox Brown, Finchley 1854.*   PLATE 17
Tate Gallery, London.

Madox Brown painted landscape at intervals during the 1850's,[1] but the quality of his achievement in this field is not always adequately recognized. These pictures, which combine a lovingly close, but never finicky, attention to detail with the largeness and breadth of the traditional English landscape school, are the most satisfactory application of Pre-Raphaelite ' truth to nature ' to landscape painting. With the doubtful exceptions of Millais and Hunt[2], most of whose best landscape painting, as in *The Blind Girl* or *The Hireling Shepherd*, is only a background for figures in which the whole interest of the picture is concentrated (in the former example, indeed, the landscape plays an essential part in the picture's 'story'), Brown seems to have been the only one of the Pre-Raphaelite inner circle really to observe and care for landscape for its own sake[3]: when he does introduce figures, they are little more than *staffage* [cf. his note on *The Pretty Baa-Lambs*: plate 12]; and the frequent references to landscape in his diary show that he did not look at it with Ruskin's 'utilitarian' or scientific preoccupations. '. . . one field of turnips against the afternoon sky did surprise us into exclamation, with its wonderful emerald tints' [Aug. 22, 1854]; '. . . out to a field, to begin the outline of a small landscape. Found it of surpassing loveliness. Cornshooks in long perspective form, hayricks, and steeple seen between them—foreground of turnips—blue sky and afternoon sun.' [September 1854. This and the following quotation refer to *Carrying Corn*.] 'It would seem that very small trees in the distance are very difficult objects to paint, or else I am not suited to this sort of work; for I can make nothing of this small screen of trees, though I have pottered over them sufficient time to have painted a large landscape, the men of English schools would say.' (Oct. 3, 1854.) '. . . one feels the want of a life's study, such as Turner devoted to landscape; and even then what a botch is any attempt to render it! What wonderful effects I have seen this evening in the hayfields! The warmth of the uncut grass, the greeny greyness of the unmade hay in furrows or tufts with lovely violet shadows, and long shades of the trees thrown athwart all, and melting away into one another imperceptively; and one moment more, a cloud passes and all the magic is gone. . . . It is better to be a poet; still better a mere lover of nature, one who never dreams of possession.' (July 21, 1855.) 'Both in the extremes of serenity and of disturbance, the clouds have a tendency to take fantastic and imitative shapes. In the most calm of beautiful days, distant pink cloudlets will move statelily along the horizon, looking like swans, like balloons, like Pillars of Hercules, like camelopards, slow, sad, and beautiful, one will follow another; then, by moments, one will alter the pose of its head, but sadly, like a ghost, or lyncanthropically change to some other animal. In stormy skies, on the other hand, we have ranges of pinnacled mountains, intersected by impassable ravines, capped by enchanted castles; with all that is wizard-like in the shape of birds, beasts, fishes, and winged reptiles, coursing in affright across the troubled and

---

[1] Ruskin made the same suggestion in 1854. 'The careful rendering of the inferior details of this picture [Holman Hunt's *Awakening Conscience*] . . . is based on a truer principle of the pathetic than any of the common artistical expedients of the schools. Nothing is more notable than the way in which even the most trivial objects force themselves upon the attention of a mind which has been fevered by violent or distressful excitement. They thrust themselves forward with a ghastly and unendurable distinctness, as if they would compel the sufferer to count or measure, or learn them by heart.' (Letter to the *Times*, May 25, 1854.)
Cf. also Rossetti's poem, 'The Woodspurge', and the section of Tennyson's 'Maud' beginning 'See what a delicate shell', which both express the same idea. James Smetham [q.v.] said of the latter that it 'answers well to an unvarying condition of a mind in anguish, viz., to be riveted and fascinated by very little things, and to have a racking sense of beauty. I remember a similar feeling on a mossy hill-top watching a silver thread of water steal through the moss alive with brilliant insects.' (Letter: 10 August, 1855.)

[1] As well as those reproduced here, *The Brent at Hendon* (1854) is now in the Tate Gallery, *Hampstead from my Window* (1857, a different view from 'the English Autumn Afternoon') is in the Bancroft Foundation, Wilmington, U.S.A., *The Hayfield* (1855), is in a private collection in England, and *Windermere* (1848-54) is at Port Sunlight. I have not so far been able to trace the whereabouts of *Southend* (1846-58, at one time in the Leathart Collection), and *View from Shorn Ridgeway* (1849-51).
[2] Besides his numerous eastern landscapes, Holman Hunt painted at least three in England in his early period: *The Strayed Sheep* (1850, Tate Gallery); the small *Blackheath Park* (Coll. Mrs. Michael Joseph, Repr. 'H-Hunt Preraphaelitism,' vol. I, p. 117), and a landscape near Helston (1860, Repr. von Schleinitz. William Holman Hunt. Leipzig, 1907, p. 74). A landscape by Millais (c. 1853), *The Waterfall*, is also at Wilmington, and I believe there was another, *The Kingfisher's Haunt*, also early, in Mrs. Street's collection, destroyed in 1941: to his later period belong two of the most remarkable *tours-de-force* in landscape painting: *Chill October* (1870, repr. J. G. Millais, vol ii, p. 27) and *Dew Drenched Furze* (1890. Repr. J. G. Millais, vol. ii, p. 295) in which manual dexterity and precision of eye are carried to a point unequalled before or since.
[3] The influence of Pre-Raphaelitism on landscape painting has not yet been fully investigated; but mention should be made of the Liverpool School, such members of which as A. W. Hunt, William Davis, and D. A. Williamson, were painting landscapes, during the 1850's and 60's, in the full Pre-Raphaelite manner. The same is true of many other landscape painters, now forgotten: to name only three at random, John Bunney, Ruskin's pupil, George, Earl of Carlisle, and G. P. Boyce.

compressed vault of heaven, or the continually increasing smoke of ten thousand pieces of meteorological artillery.' [Note on 'Winder-mere,' in the 1865 Exhibition Catalogue.]

Walton-on-the-Naze was painted in 1859/60. 'The scenery of this part of the coast is full of freshness and interest. Cliffs and ridges of clay, intercepting salt-marshes, give it a certain Dutch-English character. . . . . The lady and little girl, by their let-down hair, have been bathing—the gentleman descants learnedly on the beauty of the scene.' [1865 Exh. Cat.]

An English Autumn Afternoon, his largest and most important landscape, was painted between 1852 and 1854. The view is from the back window of his lodgings at Hampstead, where he was then living, 'intensely miserable, very hard-up, and a little mad.' When finished, it was sent to auction and fetched 'nine guineas, the frame having cost four.' This was evidently a sore point with him, but his answer to Ruskin's admittedly patronizing question, at their first meeting, 'Why did you choose such a very ugly subject for your last picture? It was a pity, for there was some nice painting in it,' ' Because it lay out of a back window!' seems an unnecessarily savage snub, and by provok-ing Ruskin's hostility, impaired Brown's prospects for several years. He described the picture as ' . . . a literal transcript of the scenery round London, as looked at from Hampstead. The smoke is seen rising half way above the fantastic shaped, small distant cumuli, which accompany particularly fine weather. The upper portion of the sky would be blue, as seen reflected in the youth's hat, the grey mist of autumn only rising a certain height. The time is 3 p.m., when late in October the shadows already lie long, and the sun's rays (coming from behind us in this work) are preternaturally glowing, as in rivalry of the foliage. The figures are peculiarly English—they are hardly lovers—mere boy and girl neighbours and friends.' [1865 Exh. Cat.]

THOMAS SEDDON

1821 London—1856 Alexandria

JERUSALEM AND THE VALLEY OF JEHOSHAPHAT, FROM THE HILL OF EVIL COUNSEL, canvas, 25 × 32, arched top.
Tate Gallery. (Purchased 1857, by public subscription organized by Ruskin, Rossetti, Madox-Brown and others, and presented to the nation in memory of the artist.)
PLATE 18

Seddon, whose father was a cabinet-maker, was obliged to spend most of his short life uncongenially employed de-signing furniture, but found time to study at the Clipstone St. School, and spent his holidays painting landscape, usually in Wales, but once, in 1850, at Barbizon. Like his brother J. P. Seddon, the architect, he seems to have been an early member of the Pre-Raphaelite circle and in 1849 is said to have occasioned comment while on a sketching tour, by declaring that three months was not too long to draw properly a single branch of a tree. From 1851 to 1853 he was painting landscapes in Wales and Brittany; in 1853 he left for the East. Seddon was not impelled to go to Palestine for the same exalted and devotional reasons as his companion, Holman Hunt: he went, partly to make up for his lack of proper training by 'novelty of motive' and observation of Hunt's technical methods, and partly to avoid being drawn back by his father into the family furniture business.

The *View of Jerusalem* took Seddon five months to paint; shortly after it was finished he returned to England, where he held a successful exhibition of his

pictures. He started again for Syria, but died in Alexandria.

It was apropos of this picture that Ruskin enunciated his curiously utilitarian theory of 'historic landscape.'

'Mr. Seddon's works . . . are the first landscapes uniting perfect artistical skill with topographical accuracy; being directed, with stern self-restraint, to no other purpose than that of giving persons who cannot travel trustworthy knowledge of the scenes which ought to be most interesting to them. Whatever degrees of truth may have been attained or attempted by previous artists have been more or less subordinated to pictorial or dramatic effect. In Mr. Seddon's works the primal object is to place the spectator, as far as art can do, in the scene represented, and to give him the perfect sensation of its reality, unmodified by the artist's execution.'

Madox Brown wrote of Seddon's pictures (Diary, Jan. 16, 1855), 'they are cruelly P.R.B.'d. . . . The high finish is too obtrusive. However, they present qualities of drawing and truthfulness seldom surpassed; but no beauty, nothing to make the bosom tingle. . . . Hunt, he tells me, gave him no advice at all; he has been prepossessed against him, I fear.' Without seeing Seddon's earlier landscapes, it is impossible to determine exactly how much the *View of Jerusalem* owes to Hunt, but comparison of it with Hunt's watercolours of Eastern landscape, done at the same time, suggests that it owes much to his example, if not to his advice. Hunt's dislike of Seddon may have been caused by the latter's high-spirited taste for violent practical jokes, which cannot have made him a comfortable travelling companion. (For an instance of this see Hunt, *Pre-Raphaelitism*, vol. I, pp. 391-4.)

JAMES SMETHAM

1821 Pateley Bridge—1889 Stoke Newington

THE FLIGHT OF PORPHYRY, pen and ink, touched with colour, 3¼ × 4.   FIG. 3
Tate Gallery, London.

Drawn in 1858. Illustrating Keats' *Eve of St. Agnes*, always a favourite Pre-Raphaelite subject.

Smetham was primarily a painter and etcher, but to-day he is only remembered for his critical articles and posthumously published letters, which show him as a man of great and original intellectual and critical ability. His essay on Blake, first published in 1868, was one of the first to estimate him at his true importance and was reprinted as an appendix to the second edition

FIG. 3. JAMES SMETHAM : THE FLIGHT OF PORPHYRY. PEN AND INK AND WASH, 1858.

of Gilchrist's *Life*. The son of a Wesleyan minister, Smetham remained all his life a devout member of that sect. He began by painting portraits; when commercial photography destroyed this means of livelihood, he became drawing-master at the Wesleyan Normal College, Westminster. The last twelve years of his life were darkened by madness, to which religious melancholia and a sense of failure and disappointment undoubtedly contributed.

Ruskin and Rossetti were both his friends, and thought highly of his work, but he attained no reputation outside his own small circle. Rossetti wrote of him:

'his work—generally of small or moderate size—ranges from Gospel subjects of the subtlest imaginative and mental insight, and sometimes of the grandest colouring, through Old Testament compositions and through poetic and pastoral themes of every kind, to a special imaginative form of landscape. In all these he partakes greatly of Blake's immediate spirit, being also often nearly allied by landscape intensity to Samuel Palmer.'

Smetham passed through a phase of Pre-Raphaelitism in the 1850's, examples of which are *Naboth's Vineyard* (1856, Tate Gallery), and the drawing reproduced here; and his close association with Rossetti, for a time during the next decade, is also reflected in his work. Neither influence was lasting (though he always owed much to the inspiration of Rossetti's personality), and in the small, highly-wrought pictures—'poetic idylls', as he called them—of his later years, many of them landscapes, there is little that is derivative. Superficially, they have not much in common with Palmer, but Rossetti's comparison shows the extent of his insight, for both are informed by something of the same mystical vision: they suggest what Palmer might perhaps have produced in the years after Shoreham, if his youthful intensity had been allowed to cool gradually into a mature serenity. If a resemblance to any contemporary movement is to be found, Smetham seems, to me at any rate, to have certain affinities with the 'minor' but authentic poetry of Dobell and Alexander Smith.

Unlike almost every other Victorian painter, Smetham improved as he grew older; the intensity of his religious life—perhaps the strongest element in his character—and the isolation in which he lived, kept him to a great extent uncontaminated by the age.

Collinson owed his membership of the P.R.B. to the persuasive advocacy of Rossetti—unable to realize that what was so effortlessly within his power was not equally within the power of others less gifted—who had been impressed by the painstaking details in his pictures, and described him as a 'real stunner' to the more sceptical Millais and Hunt. Collinson was a recent convert to Roman Catholicism, and when he fell in love with, and proposed marriage to, Christina Rossetti, who was a devout Anglican, she refused him: he reverted to the Church of England and from 1849 to 1850 was engaged to her, until a second and more lasting impulse to Catholicism led him to resign from the P.R.B. (possibly affected by the accusations of blasphemy brought against Millais' *Carpenter's Shop*) and enter Stonyhurst as a Jesuit novice. He remained there about four years until, as Rossetti put it, 'the Jesuits found him fittest for painting and restored him to an eager world', but he did not renew his acquaintance with the Rossettis and continued to paint insipid genre-pieces until his death.

Except for *Queen Elizabeth*, Collinson's pictures are Pre-Raphaelite only in their careful detail; in subject and sentiment they belong to the domestic-anecdote school of Wilkie. As Hunt said, 'with form so lacking in nervousness as his, finish of detail is wasted labour.' It was regarded with amusement as typical of him that he should have chosen to place Queen Elizabeth's Renunciation, supposed to be taking place in the early thirteenth century, in a particularly dull example of mid-nineteenth century Revived Gothic, rendered with proper Pre-Raphaelite fidelity to truth, down to the last detail of the encaustic tiling.

There must have been some hidden quality in Collinson to attract so brilliant a person as Christina Rossetti. He seems to have been chiefly remarkable for his habit of falling asleep on all occasions, which made him something of a butt among his friends, who treated him with a kind of contemptuous kindness: they describe him as 'a meek little chap . . . a small thick-necked man, chiefly a domestic painter, who began with careful and rather timid practice; in demeanour modest and retiring . . . he could rarely see the fun of anything, although he sometimes laughed in a lachrymose manner.'

JAMES COLLINSON

1825 Mansfield—1881

THE RENUNCIATION OF QUEEN ELIZABETH OF HUNGARY, canvas, 47⅜×71½, arched top.   PLATE 19
Johannesburg Art Gallery.
Exh. National Exhibition, 1851.

Elizabeth, daughter of Andreas II of Hungary, married in 1221 Louis IV of Thuringia. After her husband's death in a crusade she was deprived of her regency on the grounds that she had wasted the national revenues on charity. Having renounced her rank, she was received into the Monastery of Kitzingen, where she died. She was later canonized. This story forms the subject of Charles Kingsley's *The Saint's Tragedy*, which is no doubt where Collinson found it.

HENRY ALEXANDER BOWLER

1824—1903

THE DOUBT : 'CAN THESE DRY BONES LIVE?', canvas, 24 × 20.   PLATE 20
Tate Gallery, London.
Exh. R.A. 1856.

Very little is known of Bowler, who cannot be found to have been even remotely acquainted with any of the Pre-Raphaelite circle. He was Headmaster of the Stourbridge School of Art from 1851 to 1855, and from 1855 onwards held various posts connected with the School of Design at Somerset House. Between 1847 and 1871 he exhibited at the R.A., mainly landscapes of mountainous scenery; one or two of those exhibited during the 1850's, however, seem from their titles to belong to the same style of *genre* as *The Doubt* and were presumably under Pre-Raphaelite influence.

WILLIAM LINDSAY WINDUS

1823 Liverpool—1907 Denmark Hill

TOO LATE, canvas, 38 × 30.   PLATE 21
Tate Gallery, London.

Exh. R.A. 1859, with the following quotation:

> '. . . if it were thy error or thy crime
> I care no longer being all unblest;
> Wed whom thou wilt, for I am sick of time:
> And I desire to rest.'
> *Tennyson.*

Windus was one of the first provincial painters to be affected by Pre-Raphaelitism. A student, and later an Associate, of the Liverpool Academy, he exhibited not very interesting historical pictures there from 1845 onwards (most of which have now deteriorated through his use of bitumen), but in 1850, having seen Millais' *Carpenter's Shop* at the R.A., he returned to Liverpool a convert to Pre-Raphaelititism: his enthusiasm was largely instrumental in making the Liverpool Academy one of the most important provincial centres of Pre-Raphaelitism, particularly in the field of landscape painting.

Windus was an exceedingly slow and painstaking worker, and his chief Pre-Raphaelite pictures are only two: *Burd Helen*[1] and *Too Late*. Miller, his friend and patron, writing to Madox Brown in 1857, and presumably referring to *Too Late*, said, 'He has not yet finished the hair, but what he has done is beautiful in all eyes but his own, and it has been in and out, I should think, a hundred times'. *Burd Helen* was exhibited at the R.A. in 1856, and was very highly praised by Rossetti, and by Ruskin, who called it 'the second picture of the year', but three years later *Too Late* provoked a characteristically peevish outburst from Ruskin:

'Something wrong here; either the painter has been ill, or his picture has been sent in to the Academy in a hurry; or he has sickened his temper and dimmed his sight by reading melancholy ballads . . . a stout arm, a calm mind, a merry heart, and a bright eye are essential to a great painter . . . frequent the company of right-minded and nobly-souled persons; learn all athletic courses and all delicate arts —music more especially; torment yourself neither with fine philosophy nor impatient philanthropy—but be just and kind to everybody; rise in the morning with the lark and whistle in the evening with the blackbird; and in time you may be a painter. Not otherwise'.

Windus was evidently a man of abnormally sensitive —indeed neurotic—temperament, for Ruskin's criticism, and the death of his wife in 1862, so shook his self-confidence and nerves that he ceased to paint at all except for his own pleasure, and usually destroyed what he had painted as soon as it was finished. W. M. Rossetti (Diary, May 1862) wrote:

'Windus promised his late wife that he would never part from their daughter which prevents his entering into any arrangement that would allow of his pursuing his profession advantageously. He has lost all power of setting to work, or of resolving to do so; yet whenever he does attempt anything he finds he paints better than ever.'

One or two later works survive, of which *The Hunted Outlaw* (1861) and *The Stray Lamb* (1864), both apparently small landscapes in the full Pre-Raphaelite manner, are the most important; there are also a few small pictures, in oil and watercolour, of romantic historical and ballad subjects. On leaving Lancashire to settle in London in 1880, Windus made a bonfire of most of his studies and sketches, and his works are consequently rare.

ROBERT BRAITHWAITE MARTINEAU

1826 London—1869 London

THE LAST CHAPTER, panel, 28 × 16½.   PLATE 22
Birmingham Art Gallery.
Exh. R.A. 1863.

Martineau, who entered the R.A. Schools at a rather later age than most people, after a period spent in a solicitor's office, was little more than a *genre* painter: in spite of working for some time in Holman Hunt's studio (*c.* 1851-2), he was little influenced by Pre-Raphaelitism except in the matter of meticulous finish. *The Last Day in the Old Home* (Tate Gallery), his most elaborate work, to which he devoted the last years of his life and which he regarded as his masterpiece, is more suggestive of Frith than Holman Hunt; but the *Last Chapter* has something of the romantic intensity achieved by Hughes and Millais in their renderings of contemporary subjects.

WALTER HOWELL DEVERELL

1827 Charlottesville, Va., U.S.A.[1]—1854 Chelsea

THE PET, 33 × 22½, signed W.H.Δ.
Tate Gallery, London. (Called *Lady feeding a Bird*, in the Tate Gallery catalogue. *The Pet* is the title given to the picture by the artist himself.)   PLATE 23

THE IRISH VAGRANTS (sometimes called *Harvesters by the Roadside*), canvas, 24½ × 29⅝.   PLATE 24
Johannesburg Art Gallery.

Deverell met Rossetti in 1845 at Sass's Drawing School; from that time they were intimate friends, and at one period, from January to May 1851, shared the studio

---

[1] Repr. Marillier, *Liverpool School of Painters*, p. 248; Cook and Wedderburn *Collected Works of Ruskin*, vol. xiv, plate 1.

[1] Deverell was not an American, but his father was for a few years a classical tutor at the University of Virginia.

in Red Lion Square which was later occupied by Burne-Jones and Morris. It is curious, in view of this, and of the affectionate relations which Deverell established at once with Millais and Holman Hunt, that he was not one of the original P.R.B.'s: possibly he felt that his position as assistant master at the Government School of Design, to which he was appointed in April 1848, might be compromised by membership of a revolutionary body. He is sometimes said to have been elected to the P.R.B. in 1850, in place of Collinson (q.v.); this is not so, but his election was proposed, and if the Brotherhood had not dissolved soon afterwards, there is no doubt he would have been elected.

Deverell's working career did not cover more than five years, and he has never enjoyed the reputation he deserves. *The Pet*, which fetched only £6 6s. at the Leathart Sale in 1896, is his one well-known picture. Besides this, he painted *Twelfth Night* (1850, Coll. Mr. T. Edmondson); *The Banishment of Hamlet* (1851, owned by the artist's family, and destroyed in a fire with other works of his); *Scene from 'As you like it'* (1852/3, Birmingham Art Gallery); *Portrait of Miss Margaret and Miss Jessie Bird* (1852-3, destroyed[1]); and *The Grey Parrot* (1852-3, Melbourne Art Gallery).

The Pet was painted at Kew Green, where Deverell's family lived from 1850 to 1853. He wrote in his diary,

'The garden of this house at Kew was a great delight to me, with its vista of shrubs, trees, and flowers. . . but I fear from its coldness this studio [i.e. the conservatory in which the picture was painted] was very detrimental to my health.'

Of *The Irish Vagrants*, Deverell said, 'Rossetti seemed of opinion that . . . as the subject was so good and important I had better paint it on a larger scale.' What exactly the significance of the subject was is obscure, but it is possible to detect in it some suggestion of social criticism; Holman Hunt wrote, 'Deverell had contracted the prevailing taste . . . for dwelling on the miseries of the poor, the friendless, and the fallen.'

After his father's death in 1853, Deverell, himself suffering from a fatal disease, was obliged to support his family. There is a tragic account of his last days in a little house in Chelsea, neglected by his family, and, evidently preoccupied with the idea of death, working at his two last, unfinished pictures, *The Doctor's Last Visit* and *Young Children watching a Funeral*. Everyone who knew him spoke of him with affection, for his great talent was combined with extraordinary good-looks and charm. Considering the date of *The Pet*, its broad handling, and lack of any didactic, or even narrative, purpose are remarkable. Deverell's death may have been a greater loss than is realized: he might have succeeded, where Millais so conspicuously failed, in achieving a broader and more generalized treatment of form with no diminution of romantic and poetic quality.

---

[1] This seems to have been not unlike *The Pet*, a full-length portrait of two ladies, standing in the garden at Kew. It remained in the artist's family; the heads were cut out and framed as separate portraits, and the rest thrown away.

WILLIAM HOLMAN HUNT

1827 London—1910 Kensington

Hunt, as a young man, worked for some years as clerk to an estate agent; he then studied in the British Museum and the National Gallery, and, in 1844, entered the R.A. Schools. In 1848 he, Millais and Rossetti founded the P.R.B. In 1854 he paid his first visit to Palestine, in order to paint scenes from the life of Christ in accordance with principles of absolute historical and archæological accuracy (something of the sort had been previously attempted by Wilkie, and was later achieved by Tissot); he visited Palestine again in 1869 and 1873.

All his life Hunt remained faithful to the theories of Pre-Raphaelitism, as he understood them, and as he expounded them in his memoirs (*Pre-Raphaelitism and the Pre-Raphaelite Brotherhood*, London 1905); his later pictures are fully as detailed, but it may be said of them that they are, in fact, weighed down by their elaboration.

THE HIRELING SHEPHERD, canvas, $30 \times 42\frac{1}{2}$, signed and dated *Holman Hunt 1851 Ewell*. PLATES 25-26
Manchester Art Gallery.

Exh. R.A. 1852, with the following quotation :
  'Sleepest or wakest thou, jolly shepherd:
    Thy sheep be in the corn;
  And for one blast of thy minikin mouth,
    Thy sheep shall take no harm.'   (*King Lear*)

Painted in 1851 at Ewell, near Surbiton, where Millais was also painting *Ophelia*. A smaller version, differing in several details, belongs to Sir Thomas Agnew, Bt.

Hunt's first picture with a moral: in his own words, it was intended to be 'a rebuke to the sectarian vanities and vital negligencies of the day.' The shepherd is a type of the 'muddle-headed pastors who instead of performing their services to their flock—which is in constant peril—discuss vain questions of no value to any human soul. My fool has found a Death's Head Moth, and this fills his little mind with forebodings of evil, and he takes it to an equally sage counsellor for her opinion. She scorns his anxiety from ignorance rather than profundity, but only the more distracts his faithfulness. While she feeds her lamb with sour apples, his sheep have burst bounds and got into the corn.'

THE AWAKENING CONSCIENCE, canvas, $29\frac{3}{4} \times 21\frac{5}{8}$, arched tops.   COLOUR PLATE
Coll. Colin Anderson, Esq.

Exh. R.A. 1854, with the following quotations :
'As of the green leaves on a thick tree, some fall and some grow; so is the generation of flesh and blood.' *Eccles. xiv.18*, and 'Strengthen ye the feeble hands, and confirm ye the tottering knees; say to the faint-hearted: be ye strong; fear ye not; behold your God'—*Isaiah* (Bishop Lowth's tr.).

Intended as a 'material counterpart' to *The Light of the World*, 'representing in actual life the manner in which the appeal of the spirit of heavenly love calls a soul to abandon a lower life.' Hunt seems originally to have been inspired by the incident, in *David Copperfield*, of Old Peggotty searching for Little Emily, after she had become an outcast: but the immediate inspiration of the picture was the text in Proverbs, ' "As he that taketh away a garment in cold weather, so is he that singeth songs to a heavy heart" . . . expressing the unintended stirring up of the deeps of pure affection by the idle sing-song of an empty mind (which) led me to see how the

WILLIAM HOLMAN HUNT: THE AWAKENING CONSCIENCE (Oil, 1852-54)

companion of the girl's fall might himself be the unconscious utterer of a divine message. . . . the woman recalling the memory of her childish home, and breaking away from her gilded cage with a startled holy resolve, while her shallow companion still sings on, ignorantly intensifying her repentant purpose.'

Ruskin, in *Modern Painters*, named this picture as an example of 'painting taking its proper place beside literature.' His letter to *The Times* (May 25, 1854) explained it in detail: 'I suppose no one possessing the slightest knowledge of expression could remain untouched by the countenance of the lost girl, rent from its beauty into sudden horror; the lips half open, indistinct in their purple quivering; the teeth set hard; the eyes filled with the fearful light of futurity, and with tears of ancient days[1]. . . . there is not a single object in all that room—common, modern, vulgar (in the vulgar sense, as it may be), but it becomes tragical, if rightly read, that furniture so carefully painted, even to the last vein of the rosewood— is there nothing to learn from that terrible lustre of it, from its fatal newness; nothing there that has the old thoughts of home upon it, or that is ever to become a part of home? Those embossed books, vain and useless—they also new—marked with no happy wearing of beloved leaves; the torn and dying bird upon the floor; the gilded tapestry, with the fowls of the air feeding upon the ripened corn; the picture above the fireplace, with its single drooping figure—the Woman taken in adultery; nay, the very hem of the poor girl's dress, at which the painter has laboured so closely, thread by thread, has story in it, if we think how soon its pure whiteness may be soiled with dust and rain, her outcast feet failing in the street; and the fair garden flowers, seen in that reflected sunshine of the mirror—these also have their language—

'Hope not to find delight in us, they say,
For we are spotless, Jessy, we are pure.'

Cf. also Rossetti's *Found* [plate 33].

THE SCAPEGOAT, canvas, $33\frac{1}{2} \times 54$, signed and dated, *Osdoom Dead Sea 18 WHH 54*.   PLATE 27
Lady Lever Art Gallery, Port Sunlight.

Exh. R.A., 1856 (with a long explanatory note, paraphrasing Leviticus xvi. According to ancient Hebrew ritual, on the day of atonement two goats were taken into the temple. One was sacrificed, and on the other, the scapegoat, the sins of the people were laid, and it was driven into the wilderness in expiation.)

It is curious that Hunt should have originally thought this strange subject, so well-suited to his own tormented genius, a suitable one for Landseer. Being on the spot, however, he decided to try it himself, and encamped by the Dead Sea in a desolate wilderness of sand, salt, and rock, escorted by a few Arabs. His adventures are narrated with great spirit in the first volume of *Pre-Raphaelitism;* the Arabs were so impressed by his courage and presence of mind that they suggested on one occasion that he should become their Sheikh. A photograph exists showing him sitting at his easel with a rifle across his knees, as protection against bandits and wild animals.

The reception of *The Scapegoat* was, as might have been expected, disappointing; Hunt had intended it to convey a symbolical message of 'the Church on Earth, subject to all the hatred of the unconverted world', and illustrating the text 'surely He hath borne our griefs and carried our sorrows . . . The Lord hath laid upon him the iniquities of us all', but critics and public, with the exception of Ruskin, could only see 'a mere goat, with no more interest for us than the sheep which furnished yesterday's dinner.'

A smaller version, with a brown goat and a rainbow, is in the Manchester Art Gallery.

---

[1]This is apparently not an exaggerated description: originally the girl's face seems to have been much as described by Ruskin, but the owner of the picture, Sir Thomas Fairbairn, found it too agonizing to live with, and persuaded Hunt to modify her expression.

LONDON BRIDGE ON THE NIGHT OF THE MARRIAGE OF THE PRINCE AND PRINCESS OF WALES, MARCH 10, 1863, canvas, $25\frac{1}{2} \times 38\frac{3}{4}$, signed and dated *W.H.H. 1863-66*.
                                                   PLATE 28
Ashmolean Museum, Oxford (Combe Bequest).

THE SHIP, oil on linen, $30 \times 38\frac{1}{2}$, signed and dated *W.H.H. 1875*.   PLATE 29
Tate Gallery, London.

Painted in Jerusalem, on Hunt's third visit to Palestine in 1875, from sketches made on board the P. & O. boat between Venice and Jaffa. It was intended to illustrate the lines from *In Memoriam*

'I hear the noise about thy keel,
I hear the bell struck in the night,
I see the cabin windows bright,
I see the sailor at the wheel.'

DANTE GABRIEL ROSSETTI

1828 London—1882 Birchington

Rossetti was of Italian extraction on both sides; his father was a political refugee from Naples, his mother, though born in England, was the daughter of an Italian who had been secretary to Alfieri, and an Englishwoman. He studied at Sass's school and from 1846 to 1848 at the R.A.: in 1848 he worked for a few months under Madox Brown, and then shared a studio with Holman Hunt. He, Hunt, and Millais formed the P.R.B. in the same year.

His best work was produced between 1850 and 1862, the year of his wife's death (v. Elizabeth Siddall, plate 45). After this he became more and more of a recluse. Some of his later work was done with the help of studio assistants. In spite of the extreme imaginative intensity and beauty of his best work, he always suffered from his ignorance of technical methods; this was sometimes disastrous, as for example, in the Oxford Union frescoes (q.v. Fig. 6).

ECCE ANCILLA DOMINI (sometimes known as *The Annunciation*), canvas, $28\frac{1}{2} \times 17$, signed and dated *D.G.R. 1850*.
National Gallery, London.   PLATE 30

THE GIRLHOOD OF MARY VIRGIN, canvas, 33×25, signed and dated *Dante Gabriele Rossetti P R B 1849*. PLATE 31
National Gallery, London.

The Girlhood of Mary Virgin was Rossetti's first painting, begun in Holman Hunt's studio under his and Madox Brown's supervision during the autumn of 1848. Christina Rossetti and her mother were models for the Virgin and St. Anna. Two sonnets by Rossetti were inscribed on the frame, which elucidate the symbol in the picture:

'This is that blessed Mary, pre-elect
God's Virgin. Gone is a great while, and she
Dwelt young in Nazareth of Galilee.
Unto God's will she brought devout respect

Profound simplicity of intellect,
And supreme patience. From her mother's knee
Faithful and hopeful; wise in charity;
Strong in grave *peace*; in pity circumspect.

So held she through her girlhood; as it were,
An angel-watered lily, that near God
Grows and is quiet. Till, one dawn at home
She woke in her white bed and had no fear
At all—yet wept till sunshine and felt awed:
Because the fullness of her time was near.

These are the symbols. On that cloth of red
I' the centre is the tripoint: perfect each,
Except the second of its points, to teach
That Christ is not yet born. The books—whose head
Is golden Charity, as Paul hath said—
Those virtues are wherein the soul is rich:
Therefore on them the lily standeth which
Is Innocence, being interpreted.

The seven-thorn'd briar, and the palm seven-leaved
Are her great sorrow and her great reward.
Until the end be full, the Holy One
Abides without. She soon shall have achieved
Her perfect purity: yea, God the Lord
Shall soon vouchsafe His Son to be her Son.'

The last four lines of the first sonnet seem to refer rather to *Ecce Ancilla Domini*, which Rossetti began in October 1849. Referred to by its painter as 'the blessed white eyesore,' it was not sold until 1853. MacCracken, the Belfast shipping agent, bought it and Rossetti 'changed its name to the Annunciation as a precaution against charges of popery.'

PAOLO AND FRANCESCA, pencil, 8⅝×6¾, insc. *Dante G. Rossetti to his friend Alex. Munro.*   PLATE 32
Coll. Miss Munro.

Illustrating the story of Paolo and Francesca, as told by Dante (Inf. Canto v). Francesca, wife of Sigismondo Malatesta, son of the Tyrant of Rimini, was murdered by him together with her lover and brother-in-law, Paolo Malatesta. Dante and Virgil, seeing their spirits flying to and fro in Hell, enquire how they came there, and Francesca replies, in the lines illustrated in this drawing :

'Noi leggavamo un giorno, per diletto,
di Lancilotto, come amor lo strinse,
soli eravamo, e senza alcun sospetto.
Per più fiate gli occhi ci sospinse
quella lettura, e scolorocci il viso,
ma solo un punto fu che quel ci vinse.
Quando leggemo il disiato riso
esser baciato da cotanto amante,
questi, che mai da me non fia diviso,
la bocca mi baciò, tutto tremante.

Rossetti made three other versions,[1] all in watercolour. Two are in the form of a triptych, showing the lovers kissing; Dante and Virgil; and the lovers in Hell.
The earliest of these painted in 1855, is now in the Tate Gallery. (According to Madox Brown's diary, it was painted in a week, under the stimulus of extreme urgency, to relieve Miss Siddall, who was stranded in Paris with no money, and disposed of to Ruskin for £35. Miss Heaton had it at first, but Ruskin persuaded her to exchange it for another because, 'the subject was not suitable for a lady'.) The second was painted for Leathart, in 1862 (*Coll.* Mr. Kerrison Preston). This differs slightly in detail and is larger. The third, of the

first compartment only (*Coll.* the late Mrs. Stolterforth), though close in detail to the 1862 version, is certainly considerably earlier. Rossetti is known, from the Pre-Raphaelite Journal, to have had this triple subject in mind as early as November, 1849, but none of these early designs survive. The present drawing is always said to be dated 1854, but after the most careful examination I could find nothing on it which could be read as a date. It is so close to the 1855 watercolour as to make it very probable that it is a preliminary study, in which case it would probably, in view of the suddenness with which the watercolour was apparently begun, date from that year. Munro exhibited, at the Great Exhibition of 1851, a small group of *Paolo and Francesca*[1], which is obviously connected with Rossetti's composition: in view of the inscription on the drawing, it is tempting to assume that the sculpture was derived from it, but its style certainly indicates a later date. This group is stiffer and less sensuous than any of the existing drawings: though this is partly due, no doubt, to the physical limitations of the material, it may perhaps reflect something of the nature of the earliest studies by Rossetti, upon which it must have been based. The early drawings may have been, in relation to the later watercolours, much as the pen-and-ink *Salutation of Beatrice*, of 1849, is to the *Guardami ben, ben son, ben son, Beatrice* watercolour, of 1853.[2]

FOUND, canvas, 36×31½.   PLATE 33
Bancroft Foundation, Wilmington, Delaware, U.S.A.

Found stands outside the main course of Rossetti's development: it shows him attempting a true 'Pre-Raphaelite' picture in the manner of Millais or Holman Hunt. Apart from one or two drawings[3] *Found* is his only picture in a contemporary setting, and is his last attempt at naturalistic realism; like previous attempts it was unsuccessful, for after working on it intermittently for thirty years he left it unfinished at his death (it was actually the last picture he touched), defeated to the end by the perspective of the background. (Burne-Jones later washed the sky in with blue, and Treffry Dunn put in the bridge, etc.)
It was commissioned in 1853. Various preparatory studies exist, mostly in the British Museum and at Birmingham. One of these, a design for the whole composition, is inscribed 'I remember thee; the kindness of thy youth, the love of thy betrothal.' Jer. ii, 2. The wall, calf, and cart were painted in October and November 1854. Madox Brown wrote in his diary: 'He paints the calf in all like Albert Dürer, hair by hair, and seems incapable of any breadth . . . from want of habit I see nature bothers him.'
This particular theme was much in the air during the early 1850's and cannot really be traced to any definite source.
The story of W. B. Scott's poem *Rosabell* or *Mary Anne* is so close to that implied in *Found* that it is often suggested that Rossetti took his idea from the poem, which he and Scott had discussed and altered in June 1853. On the other hand, Rossetti's earlier poem *Jenny*,[4] and his drawing *Hesterna Rosa* (1850, Tate Gallery), which was suggested by a song in Sir Henry Taylor's *Philip van Artevelde*, both deal with a similar theme. Another drawing *The Gate of Memory* (1857) was, however, expressly derived from *Rosabell*.
The most important work of this sort is perhaps Holman Hunt's *Awakening Conscience*, 1853/4 (see Colour plate, page 29). Hunt mentions also, in this context, 'two or three pen-and-ink designs, illus-

---

[1] Mr. Marillier's statement, that another version was in the collection of Mrs. Gardner, at Boston, seems to be without foundation. The only Rossetti which Mrs. Gardner, apparently, ever acquired, is *Love's Greeting* (1861), of which the central incident is also two people kissing. A possible explanation is that Mr. Marillier was misled by a verbal description of the picture; he says that the whereabouts of *Love's Greeting* is unknown, though at the time he wrote Mrs. Gardner had already bought it.

[1] Repr. 'Art Journal. Illustrated Catalogue of the 1851 Exhibition', London 1851, p. 203.
[2] I have since found, also in Miss Munro's collection, two very early drawings by Rossetti which may be tentatively connected with this. One, in pen and brown ink, in the same style as others in the collection dated 1848, shows Francesca in a high-backed armchair, holding the book open with both hands, while Paolo, on a low stool beside her, supports the book with one hand and rests the other on the back of her chair. The other, a very rough pencil sketch, shows them both on some kind of high-backed settle; he is just about to kiss her, while she shrinks away into the corner. There are also three others, very close to the final composition of the figures, but differing slightly from it and from the sculpture, by Munro himself.
[3] The most important are *The Gate of Memory* (1857), and *Writing on the Sand* (1857, British Museum). There are also three or four pen-and-ink drawings illustrating E. A. Poe's poem *The Raven*, and one or two comic drawings, which are reproduced by Marillier.
[4] The exact dating of *Jenny* is uncertain, but W. M. Rossetti states that the first version of the poem was as early as 1850.

trating unconsecrated passion in modern life' which Millais did about this time. (*Retribution* [plate 59] is presumably one of these.) A drawing contributed in 1854 to the Sketching Club by an obscure member, Anne Howitt, presumably dealt with a similar theme, and illustrates the extent of the short-lived popularity of this kind of subject among the Pre-Raphaelites and their associates at this period: Rossetti described it as '*Castaways*, rather a strong-minded subject, involving a dejected female, mud with lilies in it, a dust heap, and other details.'

ELIZABETH SIDDALL, pen and ink, $8\frac{3}{4} \times 3\frac{7}{8}$, insc. *Hastings, May 1854.*   PLATE 38
Victoria and Albert Museum, London.

ELIZABETH SIDDALL, pen and ink, $4\frac{3}{4} \times 4\frac{1}{4}$, signed and dated *D.G.R. Feb. 6, 1855.*   PLATE 34
Coll. Francis Madan, Esq.

ELIZABETH SIDDALL, pencil, $9\frac{3}{4} \times 10$.   PLATE 35
Fitzwilliam Museum, Cambridge.

Rossetti made countless drawings of Elizabeth Siddall (q.v.). Madox Brown wrote (Diary, Oct. 6, 1854), 'Gabriel drawing wonderful and lovely "Guggums" one after another, each one a fresh charm, each one stamped with immortality.' And again, Aug. 6, 1855, 'He showed me a drawer full of Guggums, God knows how many, but not bad work I should say for the six years he has known her; it is like a monomania with him. Many of them are matchless in beauty, however, and one day will be worth large sums.'

JANE BURDEN AS QUEEN GUENEVERE, pen and ink, 19×15, signed and dated *D.G.R. Oxford 1858.*   PLATE 36
National Gallery of Ireland, Dublin.

Rossetti and Morris saw Miss Burden among the audience when they were at the theatre together in Oxford in October 1857, and persuaded her to act as a model for their decorations at the Union (see note on Fig. 6, p. 37). In April 1859 she married Morris. After his wife's death in 1862, Rossetti often painted Mrs. Morris: it is she —or rather a synthesis of her and other women with similar exotic physical attributes—that is usually called, inaccurately, the typical **Pre-Raphaelite woman.**

HEAD OF MRS. BEYER, pen and ink and wash, $6\frac{3}{8} \times 4\frac{1}{2}$.
Fitzwilliam Museum, Cambridge.   PLATE 37

This identification is due to a note by J. R. Holliday, to whom the drawing belonged: 'Study of Joan of Arc, done from Mrs. Beyer, a German woman according to W. M. Rossetti (Dante Gabriel Rossetti, I, 239.)'
Rossetti used Mrs. Beyer as a model only for *Joan of Arc*, in 1862, where the head is seen in exact profile turned to the right; but this head could very well be that of the model in *Joan of Arc*, and such a statement, coming from Holliday, must, in the absence of any positive evidence to the contrary, be accepted.
The technique of this drawing, unusual for Rossetti, is close to that of another pen and ink portrait head, that of Mrs. John Hungerford Pollen (Coll. Mrs. Arthur Pollen), dated August 10, 1857.

KING ARTHUR AND THE WEEPING QUEENS, pen and ink, $3\frac{1}{4} \times 3\frac{3}{4}$, signed *D.G.R.*   Fig. 4
Birmingham Art Gallery.

> '. . . mystic Uther's deeply wounded son
> In some fair space of sloping greens
> Lay, dozing in the vale of Avilon,
> And watching by weeping queens.'

FIG. 4. DANTE GABRIEL ROSSETTI : KING ARTHUR AND THE WEEPING QUEENS. PEN AND INK, 1857.

ST. CECILIA, pen and ink, $37 \times 3\frac{1}{4}$, signed *D.G.R.*
Birmingham Art Gallery.   Fig. 5

> '. . . in a clear-walled city on the sea,
> Near gilded organ pipes, her hair
> Wound with white roses, slept St. Cecily;
> An angel looked on her.'

Designs for illustrations to *The Palace of Art* in Moxon's illustrated edition of Tennyson, published in 1857. The actual drawing reproduced was drawn straight on to the wood-block, and was consequently destroyed when the block was cut; Rossetti's dissatisfaction with this method of reproduction prevented him from contributing, to any extent, to the revival of book illustration which reached its height in the 1860's, and in connection with which

FIG. 5. DANTE GABRIEL ROSSETTI : ST. CECILIA. PEN AND INK, 1857.

Millais and Arthur Hughes—of the Pre-Raphaelites—were particularly active.

Besides five Tennyson illustrations, Rossetti made two for his sister Christina's *Goblin Market* and two for her *Prince's Progress*; one for Allingham's *Music Master* (the famous drawing of *The Maids of Elfenmere*, which so impressed Burne-Jones), and a title-page, which was not used, for his own *Early Italian Poets*.

Rossetti gave his views on illustration in a letter to Allingham, 'I fancy I shall try the *Vision of Sin* and the *Palace of Art*, etc.— those where one can allegorise on one's own hook on the subject of the poem, without killing for oneself and everyone else a distinct idea of the poet's. This I fancy is always the upshot of illustrated editions—Tennyson, Allingham, or anyone—unless where the poetry is so absolutely narrative as in the old ballads for instance.' The St. Cecilia drawing, as engraved, certainly does show Rossetti very much 'on his own hook'. In it the angel, presumably meant to be kissing the Saint, seems to be biting her hard on the forehead. In spite of an ingenious theory, based on this and on the curious wings of the angel, put forward by Layard (*Tennyson and his Pre-Raphaelite Illustrators*), that the angel is a man masquerading as an angel with a pair of false wings (in other words that Rossetti was having an elaborate joke at Tennyson's expense), it seems more likely that the 'biting' is due to a mistake on the engraver's part. Tennyson, who was entirely indifferent to the visual arts, is said to have been very puzzled by this illustration.

THE WEDDING OF ST. GEORGE AND THE PRINCESS SABRA,
watercolour, 13½×13½, signed and dated *D.G.R. 1857*.
Tate Gallery, London.   COLOUR PLATE

Painted in 1857. This corresponds in style with five other watercolours made at this period for William Morris (all now in the Tate Gallery): their allusive, romantic titles, *The Blue Closet*, *The Tune of Seven Towers*, inspired several of the poems in Morris' *Defence of Guenevere*. Rossetti knew the *Morte d'Arthur* by 1854, but his close association with Morris in 1857 presumably influenced him in his choice of these subjects at this time: writing to Norton[1] in 1858 he said, 'these chivalric, Froissartian themes are quite a passion of mine.' This passage in a letter of James Smetham (September 1860) describes very well the characteristics of this phase of Rossetti's art: 'The Marriage of St. George is one of the grandest things, like a golden, dim dream. Love "credulous all gold", gold armour, a sense of secret enclosure in "palace chambers far apart"; but quaint chambers in quaint palaces where angels creep in through sliding panel doors and stand behind rows of flowers, drumming on golden bells, with wings crimson and green.

'There was also a queer remnant of a dragon's head which he had brought up in a box (for supper possibly) with its long red arrowy tongue lolling out so comically, and the glazed eye which somehow seemed to wink at the spectator, as much as to say "Do you believe in St. George and the Dragon? If you do, I don't. But do you think we mean nothing, the man in gold and I? Either way I pity you my friend".'

MARY MAGDALENE LEAVING THE HOUSE OF FEASTING,
watercolour, 13½×7¾, signed and dated *D.G.R. 1857*.
Tate Gallery, London.   PLATE 39

This drawing is not listed by W. M. Rossetti or Mr. Marillier. There can, however, be little doubt that it is the drawing of Mary Magdalene which Rossetti exhibited at the Pre-Raphaelite Exhibition in Russell Place in 1857. In a letter, dated July 1858, to Norton, who had been in England the year before, Rossetti wrote: 'The other picture I am doing is Mary Magdalene entering the house where Christ is, with her wicked companions trying to "chaff her out of it." This has many figures. You will remember a single figure of Mary leaving the house of feasting, for you mentioned it

too, I know.' This last description agrees perfectly with the Tate drawing. The other Magdalene subject, now in the Fitzwilliam Museum, Cambridge, is a large and very elaborate pen and ink drawing made between 1853 and 1858. There does not seem to be any connection between the two.

DANTE'S DREAM AT THE TIME OF THE DEATH OF BEATRICE,
watercolour, 18½×25¾.   PLATE 40
Tate Gallery, London (Heaton Bequest).

Painted in 1856. There are two later versions of this subject. One, made between 1871 and 1881, and now in the Walker Art Gallery, Liverpool, measures roughly seven by ten feet, and is Rossetti's largest picture: it was originally commissioned by Graham, who declined it on account of its size, whereupon Rossetti made a smaller replica, with a predella.

The subject is taken from the *Vita Nuova*, where Dante dreams that a friend told him that Beatrice was dead. The lines illustrated were translated by Rossetti:

> 'Then Love said, "Now shall all things be made clear:
> Come and behold our lady where she lies."
> These 'wildering phantasies
> Then carried me to see my lady dead.
> Even as I there was led,
> Her ladies with a veil were covering her;
> And with her was such very humbleness,
> That she appeared to say "I am at Peace".'

KING ARTHUR'S TOMB, watercolour, 9¼×14½, insc.
D.G.R., dated *1855*, copied 1860.   PLATE 41
Tate Gallery, London.

Circumstances have made it impossible to reproduce the watercolour, dated 1855, in Mrs. Huddart's collection, of which this drawing is a copy, almost certainly by Rossetti himself.

It is Rossetti's first treatment of a subject derived from the *Morte d'Arthur*; but the incident represented, that of Lancelot bending across Arthur's tomb to take farewell of Guenevere, is not found there.[1]

DANTE'S VISION OF RACHEL AND LEAH, water-colour,
13⅞×12⅜.   PLATE 42
Tate Gallery, London.

One of two subjects from Dante commissioned by Ruskin in April 1855. He gave Rossetti seven passages from the *Purgatorio* to choose from; Rossetti chose Canto xxviii, 52-55 (Dante's vision of Matilda in the Garden of Eden. The whereabouts of this drawing are not known), and Canto xxvii, 97-108 (Dante's vision of Rachel and Leah, one making a garland, typifying the *vita activa*, the other, absorbed in her own reflection in the water, typifying the *vita contemplativa*). 'Rossetti here still, painting at his drawing of Rachel and Leah. I suggested his putting in Dante in the distance and sundry great improvements.' (Madox Brown, *Diary*, August 15, 1855.)

DANTIS AMOR, panel, 19½×32.   PLATE 43
Tate Gallery, London.

Painted in 1859, but left unfinished, as part of the decoration of the settle in Morris' rooms in Red Lion Square; it was originally between two other panels, *Dante meeting Beatrice in Florence* and *Dante meeting Beatrice in Paradise*.[2]

---

[1] Another watercolour of the same group, 'Before the Battle', was done for Norton, and still belongs to his family in Boston.

[1] See Stephen's *Rossetti*, p. 40, footnote. 'While the catalogues refer to the *Morte d'Arthur* as the authority for the subject, I have not, although the first to describe the incident to Rossetti, been able to find anything about it in that wilderness of romance.' Stephen's wording rather suggests that he did not actually invent the incident, but I have not been able to trace its source. Morris' poem, *The Defence of Guenevere* is of course on the drawing, not the other way about.
[2] These were separated from the centre panel in 1865, and have passed from the Leathart Collection to that of Mr. Frank Tennant.

DANTE GABRIEL ROSSETTI: THE WEDDING OF ST. GEORGE AND THE PRINCESS SABRA (Watercolour, 1857)

The original position of this panel, implying as it does the transition of Beatrice between Earth and Paradise, suggests that it was intended to symbolize her death. This is supported by the finished pen-and-ink drawings of this subject (now at Birmingham), in which the semi-circular object held by Love can be seen to be a sundial, indicating the ninth hour, and bearing the date 12 June, 1290, the exact time of Beatrice's death. The inscription round the sun, which has the face of Christ, is balanced in the drawing by the words 'QUELLA BEATA BEATRICE CHE MIRA CONTINUALMENTE NELLA FACCIA DI COLUI', inscribed round the moon, which has the face of Beatrice. These inscriptions together form the concluding words of the *Vita Nuova*—'That blessed Beatrice who gazes continually on the face of Him *who is through all ages blessed.*' The diagonal line separating night from day has running along it, in the drawing, the words 'L'AMOR CHE MUOVE IL SOLE E L'ALTRE STELLE' (Love who moves the sun and the other stars). This line, though from the *Divina Commedia* (Par. xxxiii, 145) was connected, in Rossetti's mind, with Dante's vision of Love in the *Vita Nuova*, upon which *Dantis Amor* is obviously based: he quotes it in a note in his translation of the *Vita Nuova*, as being a parallel to the enigmatic words spoken by Love to Dante. 'I am in the centre of a circle, to which all parts of the circumference bear an equal relation, but with thee it is not so.' Rossetti interprets this as meaning that 'all loveable objects, whether in heaven or earth, or any part of the circle's circumference, are equally near to Love; not so to Dante, who will one day lose Beatrice when she dies', and, consequently intimating the death of Beatrice. In the earliest treatment of the triple subject, a pen-and-ink drawing[1] dated 1849, Love is holding a turned-down torch, another symbol of death, and the compartment is inscribed

> 'Ita n'e Beatrice in alto cielo
> Ed ha lasciato Amor meco dolente.'

('Beatrice has gone from here into high heaven, and has left Love with me lamenting.')

BEATA BEATRIX, canvas, 34 × 26, signed *D.G.R.*
Tate Gallery, London.   PLATE 44

Painted by Rossetti in 1863, the year after his wife's death, in memory of her, whose features he gave to Beatrice. He expounded it as follows:

'The picture illustrates the *Vita Nuova*, embodying symbolically the death of Beatrice as treated in that work. The picture is not intended at all to represent death, but to render it under the semblance of a trance, in which Beatrice, seated at a balcony overlooking the city, is suddenly rapt from Earth to Heaven. You will remember how Dante dwells on the desolation of the city in connection with the incident of her death, and for this reason I have introduced it as my background, and made the figures of Dante and Love passing through the street and gazing ominously on one another, conscious of the event; while the bird, a messenger of death, drops the poppy between the hands of Beatrice. She, through her shut lids, is conscious of a new world, as expressed in the last words of the *Vita Nuova*—'That blessed Beatrice who now gazeth continually on His countenance *qui est per omnia sæcula benedictus*.' (Cf. Plate 43, *Dantis Amor*.)

This is the original *Beata Beatrix*. Rossetti made altogether six replicas, two in crayon, one in watercolour, and three in oil. One of these, now in the U.S.A., which was commissioned by Graham in 1872, has a predella showing the meeting of Dante and Beatrice in Paradise.

STUDY FOR 'LANCELOT'S VISION OF THE SANC GRAEL', pencil, and pen and ink, 7 × 9⅛.   FIG. 6
Birmingham Art Gallery.

Study for a painting at the Oxford Union. Lancelot is a portrait of Burne-Jones.

[1] Now in the Fogg Museum, Harvard, U.S.A.

The buildings of the Oxford Union Society were built at the same time as the Oxford Museum, by the same Gothic Revivalist architect, Woodward. At the suggestion of Ruskin, who had been very active in the planning of the Museum, it was embellished with statues by Munro and Woolner, and Rossetti was asked to undertake mural paintings there. He refused, finding the subjects suggested, such as 'Newton gathering Pebbles on the shores of the Ocean of Truth', unsympathetic, but offered instead to organize the decoration of the debating hall—now the library—of the Union with subjects taken from the *Morte d'Arthur*.

The offer was accepted, and the decoration began in the autumn of 1857. The others concerned were Morris, Burne Jones, Hughes, Val Prinsep, Spencer Stanhope, John Hungerford Pollen, and Alexander Munro (who carved a lunette of King Arthur and his knights at the Round Table, from a design by Rossetti). Rossetti himself undertook two subjects, but only carried out one.[1] This was *Sir Lancelot's Vision of the Sanc Grael*, about which he wrote to Norton, July 1858: 'My own subject (for each of us has as yet only done one) is Sir Lancelot prevented by his sin from entering the Chapel of the San Grael. He has fallen asleep before the shrine full of angels, and between him and it rises in his sleep the image of Queen Guenevere, the cause of all. She stands gazing at him with her arms extended in the branches of an apple tree. As a companion to this I shall paint a design I have made for the purpose, of the attainment of the San Grael by Lancelot's son, Galahad, together with Bors and Perceval.'[2]

After spending about a year in Oxford, Rossetti returned to London, and the undertaking lapsed, three of the ten bays remaining unfilled. These were completed a few years later by William Riviere, a local drawing master, and his son, Briton Riviere.

In spite of the revival of interest in mural decoration which occurred in the 1840's, Rossetti and his associates, most of whom had hardly touched a paint-brush before, knew no better than to paint directly on to an exterior brick wall, covered only with a coat of ordinary whitewash. The paintings consequently perished in a very short time; they were restored in 1936 by Professor Tristram.

ELIZABETH ELEANOR SIDDALL
1834 London—1862 London

CLERK SANDERS, watercolour, 11 × 7¾, signed and dated *E.E.S. 1857.*   PLATE 45
Fitzwilliam Museum, Cambridge.

The story of Deverell's discovery of Elizabeth Siddall in a bonnet shop near Leicester Square is well known: it was perhaps his most important contribution to the Pre-Raphaelite Movement. She appears in his *Twelfth Night*, Millais' *Ophelia*, and in Holman Hunt's *Valentine and Sylvia* and *A Christian missionary pursued by Druids*, but by the end of 1852 she had become exclusively Rossetti's model; from 1850 to 1862 she appears in

[1] A highly finished pen-and-ink drawing at Birmingham of *Sir Lancelot escaping from Guenevere's Chamber*, inscribed 'Oxford 1857' is said by Mr. Marillier to be a design for a third Union subject. Coincidence of date, place, and subject support this, but against it is the fact that a third subject by Rossetti is not mentioned by W. M. Rossetti, Holman Hunt (in his monograph on the Union paintings) or Rossetti himself, who had in fact originally intended to do only one painting, until Ruskin offered to write off a debt of £70 if he did a second. Also, this drawing does not contain blank spaces for the circular windows round which the decorations were painted, such as are in the British Museum drawing for *The Attainment of the Sanc Grael*; nor does Rossetti seem to have composed it with allowance for such spaces in mind.
[2] This was never carried out, but a drawing for it is in the British Museum, and Rossetti painted a watercolour of the subject in 1864 (now in the Tate Gallery), a drawing for which is also in the British Museum. (Apart from certain differences in composition, the two British Museum drawings are so alike as to suggest that they were drawn at the same time and that Rossetti had the watercolour in mind as early as 1857.)

FIG 6. DANTE GABRIEL ROSSETTI : STUDY FOR LANCELOT'S VISION OF THE SANG GRAEL.
PENCIL, AND PEN AND INK, 1857.

nearly all his pictures. After a long and close association, lasting almost ten years, they were married in May 1860. married life was a tragedy: she became more and more feeble and melancholy, particularly after the birth of a still-born daughter in May 1861. On February 11, 1862, she was found dying of an overdose of laudanum, a drug she often took for neuralgia.

Even allowing for a certain amount of idealization on Rossetti's part, she must have been very beautiful. W. M. Rossetti describes her as 'tall, with a stately throat and fine carriage, pink and white complexion, and massive, straight, coppery-golden hair. Her large greenish-blue eyes, large-lidded, were particularly noticeable.' Millais' *Ophelia* is said to be the best likeness of her. Not only her husband, but Ruskin, Madox Brown and Swinburne thought very highly of her powers as an artist. Ruskin, wrote Rossetti in March 1855, 'saw and bought on the spot every scrap of design hitherto produced by Miss Siddall. He declared that they were far better than mine, or almost than anyone's, and seemed quite wild with delight at getting them.' Madox Brown (Diary, Oct. 6, 1854)

called her 'a real artist, a woman without parallel for many a long year.' To-day it is clear that much in her painting and poetry[1] is derivative. In her drawings and watercolours (mostly produced between 1852 and 1857, and usually illustrating subjects from romantic poetry and ballads), and in her poems, motives taken from her husband are heightened to a hectic, febrile intensity, and sometimes indeed almost exaggerated to the point of parody; even so, there remains a personal and mysteriously arresting quality in them, for which no outside influence is responsible.

It is impossible to form any clear picture of her personality. She seems to have given her confidence to her husband alone, and her few letters to him do suggest a very subdued, but individual, humour. To the rest of the world she was an enigma: she appears in the various accounts of this period, always in the background, and always quite silent, 'a shadow like an angel, with bright hair.'

[1] Fifteen poems by Elizabeth Siddall were published at various times by W. M. Rossetti: eight in *Ruskin, Rossetti, Pre-Raphaelitism*, six in his *Reminiscences* and one in his *Memoir of D. G. Rossetti*.

JOHN EVERETT MILLAIS

1829 Southampton—1896 London

Millais came of a Jersey family of French extraction. He entered Sass's Drawing School in 1838, and the R.A. Schools in 1840. He was an infant prodigy, and won several medals for drawing while still a child; his *Pizarro seizing the Inca of Peru* (Victoria and Albert Museum), is a remarkable achievement for a boy of sixteen. In 1848 he, Rossetti and Holman Hunt formed the Pre-Raphaelite Brotherhood. Technically extremely proficient, he quickly outdistanced the others and was elected A.R.A. in 1853. By the late 1850's his art had degenerated from its early promise; his later genre-pieces, sentimental and facile, were enormously popular and, together with his portraits, made him one of the most successful painters there have ever been. He achieved a baronetcy, the Presidency of the Royal Academy, and an income of £30,000 a year. Not all his later work is as bad as it is often said to be; Millais' amazing technical ability always gives it a certain distinction, and, in particular, the quality of his portraits is often very high.

MRS. JAMES WYATT, JUNIOR, AND HER DAUGHTER SARAH, panel, 17⅞×17¾, signed *JM*.   PLATE 46
Coll. Mrs. James Wyatt.

James Wyatt (1774-1853) was a prominent citizen of Oxford, of which city he was mayor in 1842-43. He had a picture and print-selling and frame-making business at his house in the High Street, No. 115, now a jeweller's, where the large hall he built for exhibitions is still in existence. He commissioned these portraits after buying Millais' *Cymon and Iphigenia* at the R.A. in 1848.

MR. JAMES WYATT AND HIS GRANDDAUGHTER MARY, panel, 13⅞×17¾, signed and dated *J.E.M. 1849*.   PLATE 47
Coll. Mrs. James Wyatt.
Exh. R.A. 1850.

A replica by Millais' brother William, with the faces and hands finished by Millais, belongs to Mr. Hugh Wyatt Standen.

LORENZO AND ISABELLA, canvas, 40×57, signed and dated *J. E. Millais 1849* (the letters P.R.B. are not part of the actual signature, but are carved on Isabella's chair).   PLATE 48
Walker Art Gallery, Liverpool.
Exh. R.A. 1849.

Begun in November 1848, and finished 'at a pace beyond all calculation' by May 1849. It illustrates these lines from Keats' *Isabella and the Pot of Basil:*

> 'Fair Isabel, poor simple Isabel!
> Lorenzo, a young palmer in love's eye!
> They could not in the self-same mansion dwell
> Without some stir of heart, some malady;
> They could not sit at meals but feel how well
> It soothed each to be the other by.'

In accordance with the exacting ideals of Pre-Raphaelite naturalism, the models were not professionals; it was felt that the artist could better achieve a lifelike portrait by painting people intimately known to him. The identification of the characters in this picture is, however, a question of some difficulty. There is no doubt that the man at the end of the table, holding a glass to his mouth, is D. G. Rossetti, or that the old man wiping his lips, and Isabella herself, are Millais' father and sister-in-law. Lorenzo is sometimes said to be William Rossetti, and sometimes Walter Deverell; the former seems more likely; Deverell was said to have been so handsome that ladies seeing him in the street used to run round another way to get a second look at him, and if he appears in this picture at all he is probably the brother whose head, which resembles portraits of Deverell, appears between the other brother's face and his wineglass. It is almost certain that W. B. Scott is the servant; F. G. Stephens is said to have been one of the sitters, but there seems to be no-one resembling very closely the undoubted portrait of him in Ferdinand and Ariel. He may be one or other of the two nearer brothers.

DESIGN FOR BOOK ILLUSTRATION, pen and indian ink, 10⅝×7⅞, signed and dated *J. E. Millais 1849 P.R.B. Coll.* The late Arthur Hungerford Pollen.   FIG. 7

This drawing is catalogued by J. G. Millais under the title *Garden Scene*. It is obviously a head piece and decorative border for a page of a book; though what book is not known. Tennyson's *Princess* has been suggested. This is a possibility; it was published in 1847, and considering the great popularity of Tennyson's poetry among the P.R.B., Millais is very likely to have read it by 1849.

STUDY FOR 'CHRIST IN THE HOUSE OF HIS PARENTS', pencil, 7¹¹⁄₁₆×13¼, signed *J.M.*   FIG. 8
Fitzwilliam Museum, Cambridge.

FIG. 7. JOHN EVERETT MILLAIS : DESIGN FOR BOOK-ILLUSTRATION. PEN AND INK, 1849.

FIG. 8. JOHN EVERETT MILLAIS. STUDY FOR CHRIST IN THE HOUSE OF HIS PARENTS. PENCIL, 1849.

CHRIST IN THE HOUSE OF HIS PARENTS (sometimes known as *The Carpenter's Shop*), canvas, $33\frac{1}{2}\times54$, signed and dated *Millais 50.*

PLATE 49-50

Tate Gallery, London.

Exh. R.A. 1850, with the title

'And one shall say unto him, "What are these wounds in thine hands " Then he shall answer, "Those with which I was wounded in the house of my friends." '

Painted 1849/50. Millais, eager for absolute accuracy, painted the figure of St. Joseph from a carpenter, in order to get the development of the muscles right; the head, however, he painted from his father. See Fig. 8

THE RETURN OF THE DOVE TO THE ARK (sometimes known as *The Daughters of Noah*), canvas, $34\frac{5}{8}\times21\frac{1}{2}$.

Ashmolean Museum, Oxford.   FRONTISPIECE

Exh. R.A. 1851.

Millais' first idea for this picture was more ambitious: 'The Flood subject[1] I have given up for this year', he wrote in January 1851, 'and have substituted a smaller composition . . . the subject is new, and I think fortunate, it is the dove returning to the ark with the olive branch. I shall have three figures—Noah praying, with the olive branch in his hand, and the dove in the breast of a young girl, who is looking at Noah. The other figure will be kissing the bird's breast. The background will be very novel, as I shall paint several birds and animals, one of which now forms the prey to the other.'

[1] The 'Flood Subject' was never carried out, but a drawing for it is in the British Museum. It represents a marriage feast with the guests heedless of the Deluge rising outside the window. Millais, who was in close contact with Holman Hunt at the time, wrote (May 1851), 'I shall endeavour . . . to affect those who may look upon it with the awful uncertainty of life and the necessity of being always prepared for Death.'

Ruskin wrote of it: 'Let the spectator contemplate . . . the intense harmony of colour in the exquisitely finished draperies; let him note also the ruffling of the plumage of the wearied dove, one of its feathers falling . . . to the ground where the hay is painted not only elaborately but with the most perfect ease of touch and mastery of effect.'

THE BRIDESMAID, panel, $10\frac{3}{4}\times7\frac{3}{4}$, signed and dated *J.E.M. 1851.*

PLATE 51

Fitzwilliam Museum, Cambridge.

Millais explained the subject as 'a bridesmaid who is passing the wedding cake through the ring nine times.' It is said to be a portrait of Mrs. Nassau Senior.

AUTUMN LEAVES, canvas, $40\frac{1}{2}\times28\frac{1}{2}$, signed and dated *18 J.M. 56.*

PLATE 52

Manchester Art Gallery.

Painted in the garden at Annat Lodge, near Perth, where Millais lived for a time after his marriage. Holman Hunt describes a conversation he had with Millais some years earlier, in the course of which Millais said, 'Is there any sensation more delicious than that awakened by the odour of burning leaves? To me nothing brings back sweeter memories of the days that are gone; it is the incense offered by departing summer to the sky, and it brings one a happy conviction that time puts a peaceful seal on all that is gone.'

THE BLIND GIRL, canvas, $31\frac{3}{4}\times21$, signed and dated *J. Millais 1856.*

PLATE 53-54

Birmingham Art Gallery.

Painted near Winchelsea in the summer of 1854; the background is a view of it from the east. The following passage, from Ruskin's *Three Colours of Pre-Raphaelitism*, conveys something of the beauty of colour and intensely luminous brilliance of this picture:

'The shower has been heavy, and is still so in the distance, where a bright double rainbow is relieved against the departing thunder-cloud. The freshly wet grass is all radiant through and through with the new sunshine; full noon at its purest, the very donkeys bathed in the raindew, and prismatic with it under their rough breasts as they graze; the weeds at the girl's side as bright as a Byzantine enamel, and inlaid with blue Veronica; her upturned face all aglow with the light that seeks its way through her wet eyelashes; a radiant butterfly has settled on her shoulder and basks there in the warm sun.'

OPHELIA, canvas, $29\frac{1}{2} \times 44$, arched top, signed and dated *J. Millais 1852.*   PLATE 55
National Gallery, London.
Exh. R.A. 1852.

The background was painted in the summer of 1851 near Surbiton, at the same time as Holman Hunt's *Hireling Shepherd*; the stream is the River Ewell.
Elizabeth Siddall, then aged about seventeen, was model for Ophelia. According to W. M. Rossetti, this picture is probably the best likeness of her.

THE EVE OF SAINT AGNES, pen and sepia ink, touched with colour, $10\frac{1}{8} \times 8\frac{1}{2}$, signed and dated *18 JEM 54.*
Coll. The late Melvill Gray.   PLATE 56

Illustrating Tennyson's poem *St. Agnes Eve.* Millais made the illustration for this in Moxon's illustrated Tennyson in 1857, but there the figure is shown, taper in hand, on a winding staircase, looking out of an open window.

STUDY FOR 'LORENZO AND ISABELLA', pencil, $9\frac{1}{16} \times 6\frac{7}{8}$.
Birmingham Art Gallery.   PLATE 57

THE GHOST, pen and sepia ink, $12\frac{1}{2} \times 10\frac{1}{2}$.   FIG. 1
Victoria and Albert Museum, London.

THE RACE-MEETING, pen and ink, 10×7, signed and dated *18 J.E.M. 54.*   PLATE 58
Ashmolean Museum, Oxford.

This was evidently inspired by a visit to the races at Epsom in May, 1853, described by Millais in a letter to Charles Collins: 'Such tragic scenes I saw on the course . . . in another carriage I saw a woman crying bitterly, evidently a paramour of the man who was languidly lolling back on the cushions flushed with drink and trying to look unconcerned at the woman's grief. This was probably caused by a notice that his losses that day obliged him to do without her society for the future.'

RETRIBUTION (sometimes known as *The Man with Two Wives*), pen and sepia ink, $8 \times 10\frac{3}{8}$, signed and dated *J.E.M. 54.*   PLATE 59
Coll. The late Melvill Gray.

ACCEPTED, pen and sepia ink, 10×7, insc. *Accepted, John Everett Millais 1853.*   PLATE 60
Coll. The late Melvill Gray.

REJECTED, pen and sepia ink, 10×7, signed and dated *J. Millais 1853*, and inscribed *Goodbye, I shall see you tomorrow* (which has been partially erased).
Coll. The late Melvill Gray.   PLATE 61

The erased inscription, in the artist's hand, does not altogether support the title 'Rejected,' given to the drawing by J. G. Millais; it may be that it was later so-called as a pendant to 'Accepted'.

The last five drawings, and three others, *The Dying Man, The Blind Man,* and *The Romans leaving Britain* (a composition later (1865) used in a painting) belonged until very recently to Millais' brother-in-law, Mr. Melvill Gray; J. G. Millais lists two others as being in the same collection, *Virtue and Vice* and *A Woman in Church watching her former Lover being married,* but these have since disappeared. They are all reproduced in the first volume of J. G. Millais' *Life and Letters of Sir John Millais* except *A Woman in Church watching her former Lover being married,* but an engraving of this, illustrating the poem 'When first I met thee, warm and young' appeared in an illustrated edition of Moore's *Irish Melodies,* published in 1856.
This group of drawings is unlike anything else by Millais; here he seems for a moment almost to approach self-revelation. What caused his temporary preoccupation with these dramatic, or lurid, aspects of passion we can only infer, but it is perhaps significant that their date exactly coincides with the period of his courtship of Mrs. Ruskin: there may also be a connection between *Retribution* and the theme of Rossetti's *Found* (q.v.) and Holman Hunt's *Awakening Conscience.*[1] Millais is also said to have made earlier drawings of contemporary subjects: Holman Hunt speaks of Ruskin being impressed by them in July 1851.

FERDINAND AND ARIEL, panel, $25\frac{1}{2} \times 20$, arched top. Signed and dated *J. E. Millais 1849.*   PLATE 62
Coll. Roger Makins, Esq., C.M.G.

The background was painted in the summer of 1849 near Oxford. Ferdinand is a portrait of F. G. Stephens; the head was painted in one continuous sitting of seven hours.
According to W. M. Rossetti (*The P.R.B. Journal*) it was originally commissioned by a dealer who declined it when finished, having 'among other things expressed some doubts of the greenness of the fairies, and wished to have them more sylph-like.'

JOHN RUSKIN, canvas, $28\frac{1}{4} \times 24$, arched top.
Coll. Sir William Acland Bt.   PLATE 72
See the note on Ruskin, page 44.

ARTHUR HUGHES
1830 London—1915 Kew Green

Hughes studied under Alfred Stevens at Somerset House, and entered the R.A. Schools in 1847. *Musidora* (1849, Birmingham Art Gallery), his first exhibited picture, was an undistinguished figure subject in the contemporary academic style, but, in 1850, he was converted to Pre-Raphaelitism (according to his own account, largely by reading *The Germ*), and met Hunt, Rossetti and Madox Brown. Millais, who seems to have had the most influence on him, he did not meet till 1852, the year in which his first 'Pre-Raphaelite' picture, *Ophelia,* was exhibited.
His best work, all produced during the 1850's, or early 1860's, maintains a constant intensity of delicate and poetic sentiment. As soon as this ran dry, his pictures become feebly sentimental and without the slightest interest: they do not even have the positive quality of vulgarity which distinguishes the bad pictures of his model. Millais, whose combination of great vitality and

---

[1] J. G. Millais, in an introduction to the catalogue of an exhibition of his father's drawings (Fine Art Society, 1901), speaking of this group, and of *Virtue and Vice* in particular, said that 'the artist's intention was to have shown by illustration the various tragedies of sin and temptation which assail the lot of man.'

technical virtuosity enabled him to succeed in spite of a similar failure of inspiration.

Hughes' extremely retiring and gentle nature, which led him, by 1858, to withdraw from London, and the assemblies of his fellow artists (up to then he had shared a studio in London with Munro), and settle with his family in the suburbs, caused him to be undeservedly obscure during his lifetime, and to-day makes the task of finding anything out about him one of great difficulty. His life appears to have been perfectly happy and entirely uneventful: in 1857 he was one of those concerned in the decoration of the Oxford Union ; in 1862 he is known to have visited Italy.

Hughes is usually classed together with such men as Windus or Deverell, artists of great but unfulfilled promise, whom circumstances prevented from executing more than one or two works: he is, in fact, one of the most important Pre-Raphaelite painters.

FERDINAND AND ARIEL (possibly the subject is *Echo, or Benedict in the arbour*, under which title it was exhibited at the Tate Gallery, 1923), panel 15½ × 11⅜, arched top. *Coll.* Mrs. Murno.   PLATE 63

This is said to be a portrait of the sculptor Alexander Munro, with whom Hughes shared a studio from 1851 or 1852 to 1858. To judge from its style, the picture was certainly painted during that period.

FAIR ROSAMUND, canvas, 15¾ × 11¾.   PLATE 64
Coll. Miss Gilchrist (on loan to the Tate Gallery).
Exh. 'Winter Exhibition' 1854.

Rosamund, daughter of Walter, Lord Clifford, was the mistress of Henry II. According to tradition he built her a 'bower' at Woodstock, which seems to have been a house in the middle of a maze of which he and she alone knew the secret; Queen Eleanor, Henry's wife, penetrated the labyrinth and 'so dealt with her that she lived not long after.'

THE TRYST, canvas, 15¼ × 11¾, signed *A. Hughes*.
Tate Gallery (Heaton Bequest), London.   PLATE 65

This picture is undated, and does not seem to have been shown at any exhibition. There is no reference to it in any published letter, either of Hughes or Ruskin—through whose agency it may possibly have been acquired by Miss Heaton. Its style indicates the early or middle fifties as its date. The features of the man resemble those of Hughes himself, as seen in his self-portrait (*c.* 1850) in the Birmingham Gallery and in Millais' *Prescribed Royalist*. The same woman also seems to occur in both versions of *Enid and Geraint*.[1]

STAGS, pen-and-ink sketch, 6 × 9½.   FIG. 9
City Art Gallery, Manchester.

An illustration to Tennyson's *Enoch Arden*, published in 1866. See note on Fig. 10.

---

[1] Both c. 1859. The smaller in the collection of Mrs. Elliott, the larger (*The Rift in the Lute*) in that of Mr. Gordon Bottomley.

FIG. 9. ARTHUR HUGHES : STAGS. PEN AND INK, C. 1866.

HOME FROM WORK, canvas, 40½×31, arched top, signed *Arthur Hughes.* PLATE 66
Coll. the late Sir George Huggins, K.B.E.
Exh. R.A. 1861.

This should not be confused with *The Woodman's Daughter*, another work of the same period also in the Leathart Collection, but disposed of some time before Leathart's death: this was not sold to a public gallery, and does not seem ever to have belonged to George Rae, who bought several pictures from Leathart at different times. It apparently represented the child sitting in the wood watching her father at work, and may have been a companion work to this picture.

THE LONG ENGAGEMENT, canvas, 41½×21½, arched top, signed and dated *A. Hughes 1859.* PLATE 67
Birmingham Art Gallery.
Exh. R.A. 1859, with the following quotation from Chaucer:

'For how myght sweetness ever hav be known
To hym that never tastyd bitternesse.'

Begun in 1853 as *Orlando in the Forest of Arden*: G. P. Boyce in his diary for March 13, 1854, records finding Hughes at work on it in Rossetti's studio. It was rejected by the R.A. in 1855, and Hughes painted out Orlando (represented as carving Rosalind's name on the tree) and substituted the present figures. A small picture, also in the Birmingham Gallery, of a woman standing alone near a tree on which is carved the name 'Amy', seems to be connected in some way with this picture; it is possibly an earlier treatment of the same theme.
Hughes wrote, in a letter to Allingham:
'Painting wild roses into *Orlando* has been a kind of match against time with me, they passing away so soon, like all lovely things *under the sun* (eh?) and as sensitive as beautiful. The least hint of rain, just a dark cloud passing over, closes them up for the rest of the day perhaps. One day a great bee exasperated me to the pitch of madness by persisting in attacking me, the perspiration pouring down my face in three streams the while—and another I had to remain for three hours under a great beech tree with roots all unearthed, and years upon years of dead leaves under his shade, listening to the rain plashings.'

APRIL LOVE, canvas, 35×19½, arched top. PLATE 68
Tate Gallery, London.
Exh. R.A. 1856, with the following quotation from Tennyson's *Miller's Daughter*:

'Love is hurt with jar and fret,
Love is made a vague regret,
Eyes with idle tears are wet,
Idle habit links us yet;
What is love? For we forget.
Ah, no, no.'

Painted 'in the garden of a Mr. Cutbush at Maidstone.'[1] A very summary oil sketch for this picture exists, showing the girl in what was evidently meant to be some sort of period costume, a full red skirt and elaborate green bodice with long sleeves; the general colour is warm, unlike the acid greens and mauves of the finished picture.
Ruskin tried without success to persuade his father to buy *April Love*, and William Morris later bought it from the R.A. exhibition while he was still up at Oxford. Ruskin wrote of it: 'Exquisite in every way; lovely in colour, most subtle the quivering expression of the lips, and sweetness of the tender face, shaken like a leaf by winds upon its dew, and hesitating back into peace.'

[1] According to Robert Ross; Burlington Magazine, xxviii, 1916, p. 171.

THE NATIVITY, canvas, 22⅜×13¼, arched top. PLATE 69
Birmingham Art Gallery.
Exh. R.A. 1858.

A companion to *The Annunciation*, also at Birmingham.

HOME FROM SEA, panel, 20×25¾. Signed and dated *A. Hughes 1863.* COLOUR PLATE, page 11
Ashmolean Museum, Oxford.

In spite of the date on this picture, there seems good reason to believe the greater part of it to have been painted at least seven years earlier.
In June 1857, at the 'Pre-Raphaelite Exhibition' in Russell Place, Hughes exhibited *A Mother's Grave*. From contemporary descriptions, it is clear that the subject of this picture was identical with that of *Home from Sea*, the only discrepancy being that in no contemporary account is the presence of the sister alluded to: in view of the way these accounts emphasize the pathetic, narrative aspect of the picture, this seems almost to prove that *A Mother's Grave* contained the figure of the boy alone. This is supported by the drawing (plate 70, dated April 1857, but inscribed *Home from Sea*, not *A Mother's Grave*).
A MS. catalogue, compiled by Mr. Charles Bell *c.* 1905, and kept at the Ashmolean, states that the landscape in *Home from Sea* was 'painted from nature during the summer of 1856, in the old churchyard at Chingford, Essex.' No authority is given for this, but in another memorandum at the Ashmolean is the information that the sister is a portrait of Hughes' wife, communicated orally to Mr. Bell by the artist; who would have been the most probable, indeed the only, source for this very categorical information about the date and *locale* of the landscape. The brilliant, fresh and minute handling is characteristic of Hughes at the very height of his powers, in the middle 'fifties, rather than at the beginning of his decline in the early 'sixties.
Finally, if *A Mother's Grave* was a different picture, it has never been heard of since.
Assuming, as all these facts together suggest, that it was not, the most satisfactory chronology for the picture seems to be: the background painted 1856; the boy's figure painted between April and June, 1857; exh. Russell Place June 1857; possibly exh. in New York the same winter (W. M. Rossetti mentions a picture *The Sailor Boy*, in the New York Exhibition, which he thought was by Hughes); the sister's figure added possibly as late as 1863.
The sister may have been added for reasons of composition, as a kind of *repoussoir*, to break up the over-dominant horizontals of the boy's figure, the edge of the shadow, the strip of sunlight, and the church. Her presence weakens the intense effect of the picture, making it less tragic and at the same time more sentimental.

STUDY FOR 'HOME FROM SEA', pen and ink, insc. *Home from Sea*, and, on *verso*, April 1857. PLATE 70
Ashmolean Museum, Oxford.

In spite of the discrepancy between the background here and in the painting, the date on this drawing suggests that it is not a composition study for the picture as a whole, but one for the figure only, after the background had been completed: not only because of the statement, presumably made by Hughes himself, that the background was painted in the summer of 1856, but also because two months seems a very short time for Hughes to have painted the whole picture.

TWO ILLUSTRATIONS FROM 'SING SONG', pen and ink, 10×7. FIG. 10
Coll. The late Thomas Lowinsky.

Though the quality of his paintings had entirely deteriorated by

FIG. 10. ARTHUR HUGHES : ILLUSTRATIONS TO CHRISTINA ROSSETTI'S
CHILDREN'S POEMS "SING SONG".

the early 1860's, Hughes' best illustrations were not produced till the end of that decade, and right up to the end of his life his illustrations retained much of their charm. In 1855 he made five delicate, but rather weak, drawings to illustrate William Allingham's *The Music Master*; and though he was not asked, the following year, to participate in Moxon's illustrated edition of Tennyson, *Enoch Arden* appeared by itself in 1866 with a cover and twenty-five illustrations by him. *Tom Brown's Schooldays* was first published in 1857 with drawings by Hughes; charming as many of these are, his gentle talent does not seem quite at home in the manly rough-and-tumble of Rugby, and it was not until the late 1860's, when George Macdonald's fairy stories began to appear in *Good Words for the Young*, that he found an entirely congenial subject. These stories, *At the Back of the North Wind*, *The Princess and the Goblin*, and *The Princess and Curdie*, and Christina Rossetti's book of children's poems *Sing Song* (1872), for which Hughes made a hundred and twenty-five drawings, are outstanding even in that golden period of book illustration.

HENRY WALLIS

1830 London—1916 Sutton

THE DEATH OF CHATTERTON, Canvas, $23\frac{3}{4} \times 35\frac{3}{4}$, arched top, signed and dated *H. Wallis 1856*.   PLATE 71
Tate Gallery, London.
Exh. R.A. 1856.

> 'Cut is the branch that might have grown full straight
> And burned is Apollo's laurel bough.'
>
> *Marlowe*.

This is the one picture for which Wallis is now known, but others painted by him during the fifties, such as *Elaine*, *Andrew Marvell returning the Bribe* and *Thou wert our Conscript* were equally Pre-Raphaelite in style, and were praised by Ruskin.
Chatterton was painted in the actual attic in Gray's Inn where the poet died; George Meredith, then aged about twenty-eight, was the model. Two years later Wallis eloped with Meredith's wife, Thomas Love Peacock's daughter.

JOHN RUSKIN

1819 Denmark Hill — 1900 Coniston

GNEISS ROCK AT GLENFINLAS, watercolour, 19×13.
Ashmolean Museum, Oxford.   PLATE 73
Drawn in 1853, to help Millais with the background of Ruskin's portrait: cf. plate 72.

THE GLACIER DES BOISSONS, watercolour, $13\frac{1}{2} \times 19$.
Ashmolean Museum, Oxford.   PLATE 74
Dated by Cook and Wedderburn 1849.

COAST SCENE NEAR DUNBAR, pen and watercolour touched with body-colour, $12\frac{1}{2} \times 18\frac{1}{2}$, insc. on rev. by the artist *Dunbar [18]57. C. saw J. R. do this*.   PLATE 75
Birmingham Art Gallery

Ruskin played an important part in the history of the Pre-Raphaelite Movement as apologist, critic, and patron, but he was in no way its originator; the principles of Pre-Raphaelitism, however similar to some of those put forward in *Modern Painters*, were arrived at quite independently, and Ruskin's first contact with the Pre-Raphaelites themselves did not take place until May 1851, when he wrote to *The Times* in their defence: his championship and patronage continued throughout the 1850's, and his great prestige as a critic hastened public acceptance of Pre-Raphaelitism.

Millais and Rossetti were the artists with whom his personal relations were closest. From 1851 to 1854 he and Millais were on intimate terms; he even infected him with an enthusiasm for architecture[1] and illuminated MSS. Millais' portrait of Ruskin was painted in the late summer and autumn of 1853 at Glenfinlas, in the Trossachs. Ruskin's interest in geology presumably influenced the choice of background—a lovely piece of worn rock with foaming water and weeds and moss, and a noble overhanging piece of dark crag; and I am to be standing looking quietly down the stream; just the sort of thing I used to do for hours together . . . we shall have the two most wonderful torrents in the world, Turner's *St. Gothard* and Millais' *Glenfinlas*. I am sure the foam of the torrent will be something quite new in art.'

---

[1] The fruit of Millais' interest in architecture was a large design for the head of a Gothic window frame, ingeniously composed of angels embracing one another, which he made at Glenfinlas [repr. *J. G. Millais*, vol. I, p. 204.]. Ruskin also tried with no success to interest Rossetti in geology and architecture, sending him, in May 1854, a piece of opal ('a magnifying glass used to its purple extremity will show wonderful things in it'), and advising him to '. . . run as far as Rouen, and look at the thirteenth-century sculptures. . . .'

Their friendship came to an end in 1854, when Ruskin's wife divorced him and married Millais. This breach was a disaster, for if Ruskin's strong ascendancy over Millais' very impressionable nature had continued, the degeneracy in Millais' art, which Ruskin was quick to detect and denounce in *Sir Isumbras at the Ford* (1857), might very well have been delayed.

Ruskin behaved magnanimously, and continued, as a critic, to further Millais' professional interests. His father was less urbane: detecting, as he thought, an intentional distortion of his son's features in Millais' portrait, he threatened to attack it with a pen-knife, so that Ruskin had to smuggle it to sanctuary in Rossetti's studio.[1]

At about this time Ruskin made Rossetti's acquaintance, and for the next ten years a large proportion of Rossetti's work was bought either by Ruskin himself or by collectors relying on his advice. Where money was concerned he was extremely generous; he offered, for example, to settle £150 a year on Miss Siddall in return for all the drawings she produced, and subsidized in 1860 the publication of Rossetti's *Early Italian Poets*. Rossetti seems at first to have disregarded the peremptory instructions on technical and other matters, which occur in Ruskin's letters; but by 1864 even he rebelled at Ruskin's continuing desire to dictate to him, and they ceased to see each other. As early as September 1855 he complained to Madox Brown that 'Ruskin had been sticking pins into him, as was his wont, for a couple of hours every three days.'

With Holman Hunt his relations were distant, but quite cordial: with Woolner, W. B. Scott, and especially Madox Brown, gruff, surly, and self-reliant natures, he did not get on at all. Although in Millais' case he put the cause of art above personal feelings, his *amour-propre* was so wounded by Brown's snub on the occasion of their first meeting (see note on Fig. 2) that he never mentioned any picture of Brown's in his critical writings, and even went so far as to tell a wealthy collector 'Do not buy any Madox Brown at present. . . . do you not see his name never occurs in my books?' Ruskin's hostility was undoubtedly one of the reasons for Brown's poverty and failure during the 1850's.

As a draughtsman, Ruskin was well grounded in the principles of the English landscape school: Roberts, de Wint, Harding, Prout and Turner were among the artists whose drawings his father bought, and from whom he received occasional instruction; his earliest drawings, carefully composed 'picturesque' subjects, reflect this influence. In the innumerable drawings he produced from *c.* 1845 onwards, detailed studies of architecture, clouds, flowers, trees, shells, rocks (a passionate geologist, he collected minerals with the same enthusiasm as he

did missals or Turner's drawings), and landscapes, of almost everything, in short, except the human figure, there is no attempt at composition or selection. 'I have no power of design' he once wrote, 'I can only paint what I see.' Given this limitation, his drawings are unsurpassed for delicacy of touch and exquisite sensitiveness of eye and hand.

FREDERIC GEORGE STEPHENS
1828 London—1907 Hammersmith

MOTHER AND CHILD, canvas, $18\frac{1}{2} \times 25\frac{1}{4}$, arched top, signed *F.G.S.*   PLATE 76
Tate Gallery, London.

Of the very few surviving pictures by Stephens,[1] this is undoubtedly the best. A fellow-student of Holman Hunt's at the R.A. Schools, Stephens was one of the seven original Pre-Raphaelite Brothers; but exaggeratedly high standards and a too-active critical faculty led him, by the early 1850's, to give up painting altogether. He became an art critic of an erudite and scholarly kind, publishing, besides an article in the *Athenæum* almost every week from 1861 to 1901, various *catalogues raisonnés*, and, in the *Portfolio* in 1894, an important monograph on Rossetti.

JOHN BRETT, A.R.A.
1830 Bletchingley—1902 Putney

THE STONEBREAKER, canvas, $19\frac{1}{2} \times 26\frac{7}{8}$, signed and dated *John Brett 1857-8*.   PLATE 77
Walker Art Gallery, Liverpool.
Exh. R.A. 1858.
Painted at Box Hill, near Dorking.

FEBRUARY IN THE ISLE OF WIGHT, watercolour and bodycolour, $15\frac{3}{4} \times 13\frac{7}{16}$, signed and dated *John Brett 1866*.
Birmingham Art Gallery.   PLATE 78

THE VAL D'AOSTA, canvas, $34\frac{1}{2} \times 26\frac{7}{8}$, signed and dated *John Brett 1858*.   PLATE 79
Coll. Sir William Cooper, Bt.
Exh. R.A. 1859.

Brett was one of the very few painters to be seriously—and in his case, disastrously—influenced by the advice of Ruskin. He entered the R.A. Schools in 1854, and must shortly afterwards have been influenced by Pre-Raphaelitism, and in contact with the Pre-Raphaelites themselves, for he exhibited a portrait of Mrs. Coventry Patmore at the R.A. in 1856, and in 1857 was represented at the Pre-Raphaelite Exhibition in Russell Place.

---

[1] Ruskin's lip had been bitten by a dog when he was a child, and he was something of a problem to the portrait painter. Woolner, writing of Millais' pencil drawing of the head for this portrait, said 'the likeness was very good, but the expression was that of a hyena, or something between Carker and that hilarious animal.' ('Carker' was presumably the villain of Dickens' *Dombey and Son*. As represented by 'Phiz', he is not unlike Ruskin.) This is curiously like Madox Brown's description of Ruskin as 'in appearance a cross between a demon and a tallow-chandler.'

[1] They are all now in the Tate Gallery, and include (as well as two small drawings and two small and unimportant portraits) an unfinished *Morte d'Arthur* and a highly finished, rather laborious, mediæval subject, *The Proposal*. Stephens often used to declare 'with satisfaction' that he had destroyed *all* his paintings, but these two, and *Mother and Child*, were discovered after his death, hidden in a lumber-room.

The Stonebreaker (a view of Box Hill, near Dorking) made his reputation: with the *Val d'Aosta*, it is one of the most remarkable instances of the application of strict Pre-Raphaelite principles to landscape painting. Ruskin singled it out for particular praise, adding a very characteristic remark, 'If he can make so much of chalk flint, what will he not make of mica slate, or gneiss?' and when Brett was at work in the Val d'Aosta, Ruskin, who was staying at Turin, '. . . sent for him because . . . I thought he wanted some lecturing, like Inchbold . . . he is much tougher and stronger and takes more hammering; but I think he looks more miserable every day, and I have good hope of making him completely wretched in a day or two more.'

It would be interesting to know what Brett thought of this treatment: the fact that it was all too successful is obvious from the picture itself. Ruskin, who bought it, was fully aware of its deficiencies: in a critical note, too long to be printed in full here, he elaborated his theory of 'historic landscape' (cf. Plate 18).

'Here we have, by the help of art, the power of visiting a place, reasoning about it, and knowing it, as if we were there. . . . I never saw the mirror so held up to Nature, but it is Mirror's work, not Man's . . . yet precious in its patient way; and, as a wonder of toil and delicate handling, unimpeachable . . . the chestnut trees are like a finished design of Dürer's—every leaf a study; the poplar trunks and boughs drawn with an unexampled exquisiteness of texture and curve.'

Twenty years later his comment was more ambiguous:

'In good, permanent, and honourably finished oil painting this picture cannot be surpassed; it is as safe as a piece of china, and as finished as the finest engraving.'

Ruskin's 'hammering' and the sustained effort necessary to produce such a *tour de force* as the *Val d'Aosta*, seem to have had the same effect on Brett as overwinding on a watch: it is as though some spring inside him were broken, for he never again achieved anything at all comparable to *The Stonebreaker* or the *Val d'Aosta*. His style did not, as one might expect, broaden and become more soft; his later pictures, often of sea-shore subjects, are remarkable for their dryness and insensitive elaboration of detail. His interest in detail probably springs as much from scientific curiosity as from æsthetic theory, for he was a distinguished scientific amateur, and became a Fellow of the Royal Astronomical Society: in this he showed himself a true disciple of Ruskin.

EDWARD COLEY BURNE BURNE-JONES

1833 Birmingham—1898 Fulham

Burne-Jones was originally intended for the Church, and entered Exeter College, Oxford, in 1852. Here he met William Morris, and they, with others including the poet R. W. Dixon, were concerned in the publication of *The Oxford and Cambridge Magazine*, in which some of Morris' early writings, as well as contributions by Rossetti, appeared. In 1855 Burne-Jones was much impressed by some drawings by Rossetti in Combe's

collection in Oxford: at the end of the same year he met Rossetti, and on his advice left the University to take up painting. He received a few lessons from Rossetti (or rather, was allowed to watch Rossetti at work), but was otherwise self-taught. His earliest work is very strongly under Rossetti's influence. In 1859 and 1862 he visited Italy, and his later work reflects the influence of Italian fifteenth-century masters, particularly Botticelli and Mantegna.

THE MAGIC CIRCLE, watercolour, $27\frac{1}{4} \times 20\frac{1}{2}$.   PLATE 80
Tate Gallery, London.

Probably painted *c*. 1880.

CLERK SANDERS, watercolour, $27 \times 16\frac{1}{2}$, signed and dated *E.B.J. 1861*.   PLATE 81
Tate Gallery, London.

One of Burne-Jones' earliest watercolours, belonging to a period when Rossetti's influence was at its strongest. Illustrating the ballad of *Clerk Sanders*: 'Clerk Sanders entreating Maid Margaret to let him in to her house, while she faintly repels him.'

KING COPHETUA AND THE BEGGAR MAID, canvas, $115\frac{1}{2} \times 53\frac{1}{2}$, signed and dated *E.B.J. 1884*.   PLATE 82
Tate Gallery, London.

The legend of King Cophetua, a King of Africa, who married a beggar-girl called Penelophen, is the subject of a ballad in the Percy Collection, and also of Tennyson's poem *The Beggar Maid*. Burne-Jones started a painting of this subject in 1862, but it was never finished; this is also in the Tate Gallery.

AURORA, canvas, $70\frac{1}{2} \times 30$, signed and dated *E.B.J. 1896*.   PLATE 83
Coll. The late Lady Desborough.

Lady Burne-Jones states that the background is based on a drawing of the canal at Oxford, made in 1867; there is still a view of the canal, from one of the bridges near the Station, which is reminiscent of this picture.
Burne-Jones wrote of it, on seeing it hung at the New Gallery: 'It looked more like a pale watercolour among the rest; it most certainly cannot scream, its voice was like the faint sound of a flute that can hardly be heard among the cornets-a-piston.'

THE ARMING OF PERSEUS, tempera on canvas, 60×50.
                                        PLATE 84
Corporation of Southampton (Southampton Civic Centre).

THE CALL OF PERSEUS, tempera on canvas, 60×50.
                                        PLATE 85
Corporation of Southampton (Southampton Civic Centre).

Two full-sized preparatory studies for the *Perseus* series which were commissioned by the Rt. Hon. Arthur Balfour (later first Earl of Balfour) in 1875, as decorations for his dining room in Carlton House Terrace: these were not all carried out, but those that were are in the possession of the present Earl. Ten small studies in watercolour are in the Tate Gallery, and the ten full-sized studies, purchased after the artist's death by Lord Faringdon—who also owned the *Briar Rose* series—now belong to the Corporation of Southampton.

STUDY OF ARMOUR, body colour, $21 \times 14\frac{1}{4}$.　PLATE 86
Fitzwilliam Museum, Cambridge.

Made in connection with one of the *Perseus* series.
Much of the armour in Burne-Jones later pictures was designed by
the artist himself, 'on purpose to lift it out of association with any
historical period', and armour was actually made according to
some of these designs.
Burne-Jones may have got this idea from Morris when they were in
Oxford together in 1857. Morris is known to have had armour made
for him then, but always in a spirit of the most scientific accuracy:
this epitomizes the contrast between the dreamy mediævalism of
Burne-Jones, who used the Middle Ages as a mine of vague romantic
and poetic motives, and Morris' matter-of-fact, but in its results no
less poetic, curiosity about the practical details of mediæval life.
Burne-Jones and Morris took turns to draw one another wearing
the armour, when they were engaged on their paintings at the
Union. According to Burne-Jones it consisted of a coat of mail and
a helmet, made, very well, by a local blacksmith. Prinsep's version
of the story is that Morris at first tried to make a suit of chain-mail
himself, and dressed a man up in it, to be photographed in various
positions: he had not realized that the links should be smaller inside
the knees and elbows, *and* the man was unable to move; it was after
this that the blacksmith was called in.

A ZITHERN PLAYER, black, bronze, and gold ink, on paper
tinted dark brown, $13\frac{3}{4} \times 7\frac{7}{8}$, signed and dated *E.B-J.
1896*.　PLATE 87
Tate Gallery, London.

THE SLEEPING KNIGHTS IN THE BRIARWOOD, canvas,
$24 \times 32\frac{1}{2}$.　PLATE 88
Walker Art Gallery, Liverpool.

This is a preparatory study from the nude for the first picture of
the Briar Rose series, *The Coming of the Prince*, probably made c. 1870.
The figure of the Prince, which would be on the extreme left, is
omitted here. There are two versions of the Briar Rose; the smaller
(1870-73), originally in the Graham Collection, now in that of Mrs.
Raymond Asquith, the larger (begun about 1870 and finished 1890)
in the collection of Viscount Faringdon.

THE GARDEN OF PAN, canvas, $30\frac{3}{4} \times 46$.　PLATE 89
The Lady Lever Art Gallery, Port Sunlight.

Painted in 1886-87 (another version is said to be in Australia).

SHEET OF STUDIES, watercolour, $11\frac{7}{8} \times 18\frac{1}{2}$. Signed and
dated *E. Jones 1860*.　PLATE 90
Fitzwilliam Museum, Cambridge.

Studies for the decorations in William Morris' house, 'The Red
House', Bexley Heath. Fairfax Murray, who owned the drawing,
stated that the seated figure was drawn from Morris.

GREEN SUMMER, watercolour and body colour, $11\frac{1}{2} \times 19$,
signed and dated *E.B.J. 1864*.　PLATE 91
Coll. C. B. Coltart, Esq.

Painted when Burne-Jones was staying with William Morris at
the Red House, Bexley, Kent. A larger version in oil, dated 1868,
belongs to Viscountess Milner.

GOING TO THE BATTLE, pen and ink on vellum, $8\frac{7}{8} \times 7\frac{11}{16}$.
Fitzwilliam Museum, Cambridge.　FIG. 11

One of a number of similar pen and ink drawings made between
1856 and 1859, at a time when Burne-Jones' weak health often
prevented him from attempting anything on a larger scale.
These are almost his earliest known works, but the exact course of

FIG. 11. EDWARD BURNE-JONES : GOING TO THE BATTLE.
PEN AND INK, 1858.

his early development is still rather obscure. It was not till 1854
that he 'first intended to cultivate drawing to some extent', and from
1854 to 1856 he was engaged in making illustrations for Archibald
Maclaren's book of children's poems *The Fairy Family*. These have
considerable charm, but are quite immature, and would not be easily
recognized as being from the same hand as the pen and ink drawings
of a few years later.[1] Burne-Jones refused to admit them into the
canon of his work, and the first work to be so admitted was *The
Waxen Image* of 1856 (Coll. the late Mrs. Street, destroyed 1941),
a pen-and-ink drawing of the same type as *Going to the Battle*. There
were probably others made at this period which have not survived,
for Rossetti writes (June 1856) of Burne-Jones' 'designs' and speaks
of them again in February 1857 as 'marvels in finish and imaginative
detail, unequalled by anything except perhaps Albert Dürer's
finest work', and no drawings of this sort, except *The Waxen Image*,
seem to be dated earlier than 1858.
The comparison with Dürer is significant. The inspiration of
Rossetti's 'Froissartian' watercolours is obvious in this group of
drawings (indeed the similarity between this particular drawing
and Rossetti's watercolour *Before the Battle*, also dated 1858, is too
close to be a coincidence), but the finicky pen-work, stiffer, dryer,
and more timid than anything by Rossetti, and the elaborate
hatching with which every corner of the paper is filled, suggests that
Burne-Jones was influenced in his technique by the study of engravings: the style of the architecture in the background suggests
early German engravings in particular, and he is known to have
been interested in Dürer at this period, for he mentions him several
times in letters. In 1857 he wrote that his and Morris' rooms in Red
Lion Square were 'hung with brasses of old knights and drawings of
Albert Dürer'; in April 1859, writing to a child, he said 'how long
before we bring out a picture book together . . . and make people
say that Albert Dürer has come back again?'

---

[1] Lady Burne-Jones reproduces two of these drawings (vol. i, p. 120). The
illustrations were never finished, and when *The Fairy Family* appeared in 1857,
it was with only a title page and frontispiece engraved on steel, and a tail-piece
on wood, full of the most exquisitely minute and fanciful detail. Burne-Jones'
dislike of his own early productions apparently extended even to the very
beautiful, and entirely characteristic, wood engraving *Summer Snow* (*Good
Words*, May 1863.)

SIMEON SOLOMON

1840 London—1905 London

DANTE'S FIRST MEETING WITH BEATRICE, pen and ink, 7⅜×9, signed and dated *S. 12/9/59-63.*   FIG. 12
Tate Gallery, London.

Simeon Solomon, like Swinburne, was one of the principal links connecting the art of Rossetti with the 'Aesthetic' movement. He was an orthodox Jew, and many of his early paintings and drawings, in which Rossetti's influence is apparent, are of subjects from the Old Testament and scenes of Jewish ceremonial; by the late 'sixties he was also painting classical subjects, influenced by such Italian painters as Luini, Boltraffio, and Leonardo, whose works he saw on his visits to Italy in 1866 and 1869, and also perhaps affected by his association at this period with Swinburne and Walter Pater. His incoherent, but in places beautiful, prose-poem, *A Vision of Love Revealed in Sleep*, must also owe something to this association.

Swinburne published an essay on Solomon in 1871, which was not reprinted. This manages to suggest something of the combination of sensuousness and mysticism which are the characteristics of Solomon's art at its best:

'Grecian form and beauty divide the allegiance of his spirit with Hebrew shadow and majesty; depths of cloud unsearchable and summits unsurmountable of fire darken and lighten before the vision of a soul enamoured of soft light and clear water, of leaves and flowers and limbs more lovely than these.'

In the early 1870's Solomon gave way to drink and dissipation. His friends made various attempts to reform him, with no success: he continued to live a jovial and unrepentant life in the London underworld, sometimes in the workhouse, sometimes earning a few shillings as a pavement artist or by making innumerable and entirely worthless, sanguine drawings of heads, much to the detriment of his subsequent reputation.

FIG. 12. SIMEON SOLOMON : DANTE'S FIRST MEETING WITH BEATRICE. PEN AND INK.

WILLIAM MORRIS

1834 Walthamstow—1896 Hammersmith

LA BELLE ISEULT (sometimes known as *Queen Guenevere*),
canvas, 28⅛×20.   PLATE 92
Tate Gallery, London.

STUDY FOR AN EPISODE IN 'THE LEGEND OF ST. GEORGE',
pen and ink.   PLATE 93
Victoria and Albert Museum, London.

Morris' career as a painter was short: Rossetti, declaring
that 'the man who has any poetry in him ought to
paint it; the next Keats ought to be a painter', persuaded
him, towards the end of 1856, when he was still articled
to Street, to abandon architecture for painting. In
June 1857 Rossetti wrote to W. B. Scott 'Morris has as
yet done nothing in art, but is now busily painting his
first picture "Sir Tristram, after his illness, in the garden
of King Mark's palace, recognised by the dog he had
given to Iseult", it is all being done from nature of course,
and I believe will turn out capitally.' This picture was
commissioned by Plint for £70, but was very much
altered under the supervision of Madox Brown, and
never finished; it is not known what became of it, nor
of Morris' only recorded watercolour, also made in
1857, which illustrated a subject from the *Arabian Nights*,
The Soldan's Daughter in the Palace of Glass, and in which,
according to Mackail, 'the Soldan's Daughter was seated
in a heavy armchair, probably studied from one of those
at Red Lion Square, and the Palace was in all shades of
bluish glass.'
In the same year, Morris was one of those concerned with
the decoration of the Oxford Union. He chose as his
subject, 'Sir Palomides watching Tristram and Iseult'.
According to Prinsep, it was
'artistically not unpleasant, for Morris had a genius for decoration;
but the details were monstrous. . . . the drawing of the faces and
hands were what you would expect from a man who had never paid
any attention to drawing. The figures, had you seen them, would
have been fourteen feet high, but happily he covered all but the
upper parts with sunflowers. What was seen was comic enough.'
The formal pattern with which Morris covered the
ceiling of the room was the most successful part of the
whole undertaking, and showed even then that his talent
lay in the direction of applied art. *La Belle Iseult*, the only
easel picture of Morris' now known, was painted in
Oxford in 1858, and is a portrait of Jane Burden (see
also plate 36). While engaged on this picture, Morris
is traditionally said to have written 'I cannot paint
you, but I love you' on his drawing, and to have shown
it to her. He married her in April 1859, and the impulse
to paint—at any rate as far as easel pictures were
concerned—seems to have come to an end; though he did

paint the doors of a cabinet, which Philip Webb made
c. 1861, with the legend of St. George. The drawing
reproduced is a study for one of these panels.

FREDERIC LEIGHTON, LORD LEIGHTON

1830 Scarborough—1896 Kensington

A LEMON TREE, pencil, 21×15½, signed and dated
L.59 Capri.   PLATE 94
Coll. Mrs. Richard Huddart.

Leighton spent his formative years on the Continent,
being hurried from one Academy of Art to another;
this prevented him from being drawn into the Pre-
Raphaelite circle of influence, as would probably have
happened if he had been sent to the R.A. Schools in
the ordinary way. He visited London in 1849, but his
letters home contain no mention of the Pre-Raphaelite
pictures at the Academy, and his reference to 'a new
school in England, and a very promising one; correctly
drawn historical *genre* seems to me the best definition
of it', seems from the context to refer rather to the work of
Goodall, Ward, and Frith. In any case, Leighton later, in
1856, repudiated any connection with Pre-Raphaelitism
—'I told them (Millais, Holman Hunt and Rossetti) that
I was wholly opposed to their views.' Though he was
abroad from 1849 to 1856, a slight Pre-Raphaelite
tinge can be detected in such pictures of this period as
Cimabue's Madonna and *The Death of Brunelleschi*: this
can be explained by his years of study under the
'Nazarene', Steinle.
The Lemon Tree is the most important of a group of
drawings made at intervals during the 1850's, now
mostly in the Leighton House Museum, Kensington, the
British Museum, and Mrs. Huddart's collection. They
are for the most part studies of flowers and foliage, with
one or two details of architecture and studies of heads, in
the same meticulous style, having no relation at all to that
of Leighton's other drawings. That they perhaps owe
something to the teaching of Ruskin, who was later
enthusiastic in their praise, is suggested by a passage
in a letter of Leighton's dated at the end of 1852,
'I long to find myself again face to face with Nature, to
follow it, to watch it, and to copy it, closely, faithfully,
ingeniously, as Ruskin suggests—"choosing nothing and
rejecting nothing",' and by comparison of Ruskin's
illustrations of architectural details in *The Stones of
Venice* with similar drawings by Leighton such as the
famous *Byzantine Well-Head* dated 1852 (repr. Rhys p. 6;
Barrington, Vol. I, p. 80), also in Mrs. Huddart's
collection.

PLATES

1. WILLIAM BELL SCOTT : IRON AND COAL (Oil, c. 1855-60)

2. DETAIL OF PLATE 1

3. DETAIL OF PLATE 1

4. WILLIAM DYCE : PEGWELL BAY (Oil, 1858-60)

5. WILLIAM DYCE: GEORGE HERBERT AT BEMERTON (Oil, 1861)

6. AUGUSTUS LEOPOLD EGG : CROMWELL BEFORE NASEBY (Oil, 1859)

7. FORD MADOX BROWN : WORK (Oil, 1852-65)

8. DETAIL OF PLATE 7

9. DETAIL OF PLATE 7 (CARLYLE AND F. D. MAURICE)

10. DETAIL OF PLATE 7

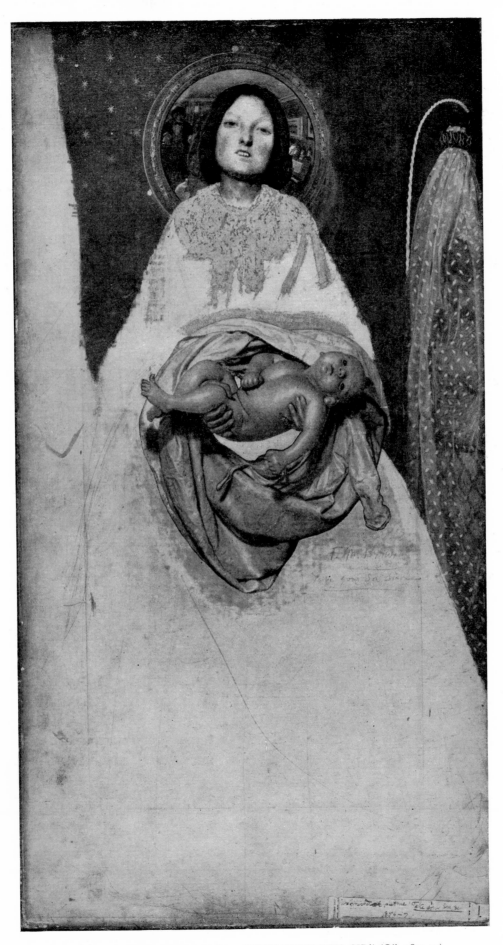

11. FORD MADOX BROWN : "TAKE YOUR SON, SIR" (Oil, 1851-57)

12. FORD MADOX BROWN : THE PRETTY BAA-LAMBS (Oil, 1851-59)

13. FORD MADOX BROWN : THE TRAVELLER (Watercolour and bodycolour, 1868)

14.   FORD MADOX BROWN : DETAIL OF "AN ENGLISH AUTUMN AFTERNOON" (See Fig. 2) (Oil, 1852-54)

15. FORD MADOX BROWN : THE LAST OF ENGLAND (Oil, 1852-55)

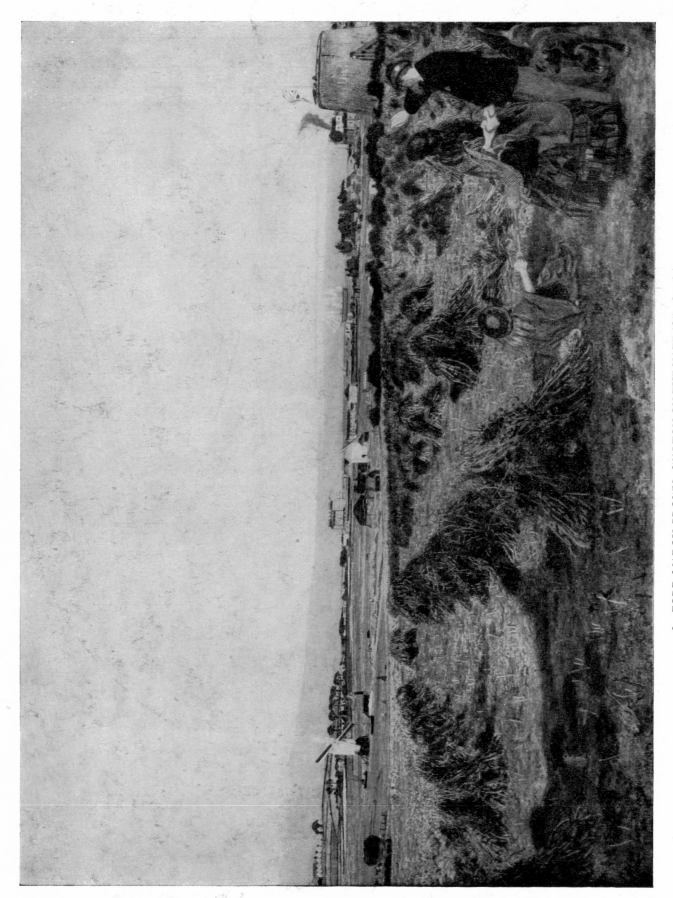

16. FORD MADOX BROWN : WALTON-ON-THE-NAZE (Oil, 1859-60)

17. FORD MADOX BROWN : CARRYING CORN (1854)

18. THOMAS SEDDON : JERUSALEM AND THE VALLEY OF JEHOSHAPHAT, FROM THE HILL OF EVIL COUNSEL (Oil, 1854)

19. JAMES COLLINSON : THE RENUNCIATION OF QUEEN ELIZABETH OF HUNGARY (Oil, 1850-51)

20. HENRY ALEXANDER BOWLER : THE DOUBT—"CAN THESE DRY BONES LIVE?" (Oil, 1856)

21. WILLIAM LINDSAY WINDUS : "TOO LATE" (Oil, 1857-59)

22. ROBERT BRAITHWAITE MARTINEAU : THE LAST CHAPTER (Oil, 1863)

23. WALTER HOWELL DEVERELL : THE PET (Oil, 1852-53)

24. WALTER HOWELL DEVERELL : THE IRISH VAGRANTS (Oil, 1853)

25. WILLIAM HOLMAN HUNT : THE HIRELING SHEPHERD (Oil, 1851)

26. DETAIL OF PLATE 25

27. WILLIAM HOLMAN HUNT : THE SCAPEGOAT (Oil, 1854)

28.   WILLIAM HOLMAN HUNT : LONDON BRIDGE ON THE NIGHT OF THE MARRIAGE OF THE PRINCE AND PRINCESS OF WALES, MARCH 10, 1863 (Oil, 1863-66)

29. WILLIAM HOLMAN HUNT : THE SHIP (Oil, 1875)

30. DANTE GABRIEL ROSSETTI : "ECCE ANCILLA DOMINI" (Oil, 1849-53)

31. DANTE GABRIEL ROSSETTI : THE GIRLHOOD OF MARY VIRGIN (Oil, 1848-51)

32. DANTE GABRIEL ROSSETTI : PAOLO AND FRANCESCA (Pencil, 1855)

35. DANTE GABRIEL ROSSETTI : ELIZABETH SIDDALL (Pencil)

36.   DANTE GABRIEL ROSSETTI : JANE BURDEN AS QUEEN GUENEVERE (Pen and ink, 1858)

37. DANTE GABRIEL ROSSETTI : MRS. BEYER (Pen and ink and wash)

38. DANTE GABRIEL ROSSETTI : ELIZABETH SIDDALL (Pen and ink, 1854)

41. DANTE GABRIEL ROSSETTI : ARTHUR'S TOMB (Copy; dated 1860, of a watercolour dated 1854)

42.   DANTE GABRIEL ROSSETTI : DANTE'S VISION OF RACHEL AND LEAH (Watercolour, 1855)

43. DANTE GABRIEL ROSSETTI : DANTIS AMOR (Oil, 1859)

44. DANTE GABRIEL ROSSETTI : BEATA BEATRIX (Oil, 1863)

45. ELIZABETH ELEANOR SIDDALL : CLERK SANDERS (Watercolour, 1857)

46. JOHN EVERETT MILLAIS : MRS. JAMES WYATT, JUN., AND HER DAUGHTER SARAH (Oil, 1849)

47. JOHN EVERETT MILLAIS : JAMES WYATT AND HIS GRAND-DAUGHTER MARY (Oil, 1849)

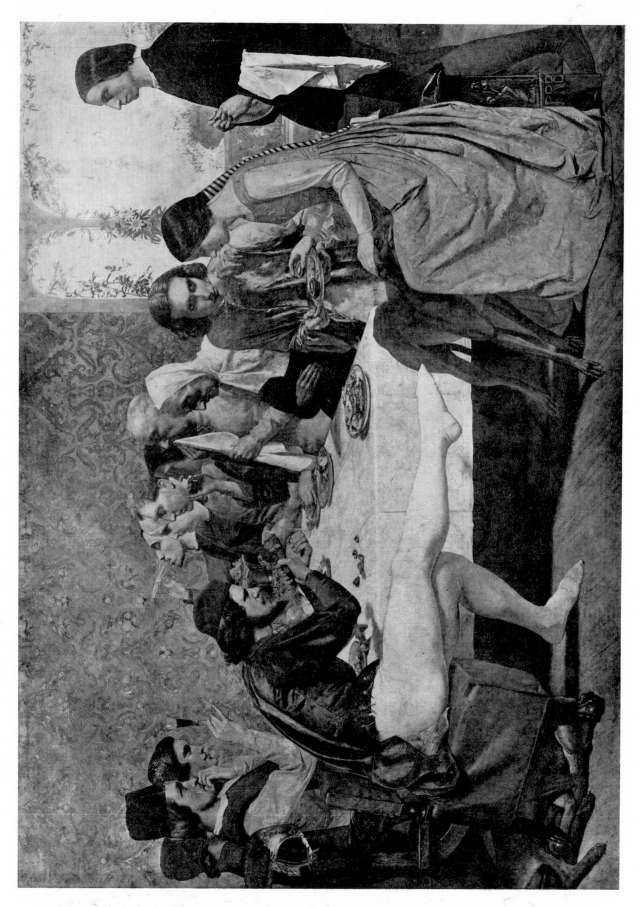

48. JOHN EVERETT MILLAIS : LORENZO AND ISABELLA (Oil, 1848-49)

49. JOHN EVERETT MILLAIS : CHRIST IN THE HOUSE OF HIS PARENTS (Oil, 1849-50)

50. DETAIL OF PLATE 49

51. JOHN EVERETT MILLAIS : THE BRIDESMAID (Oil, 1851)

52. JOHN EVERETT MILLAIS : AUTUMN LEAVES (Oil, 1856)

53. JOHN EVERETT MILLAIS : THE BLIND GIRL (Oil, 1854-56)

54. DETAIL OF PLATE 53

55. JOHN EVERETT MILLAIS : OPHELIA (Oil, 1851-52)

56. JOHN EVERETT MILLAIS : THE EVE OF ST. AGNES (Pen and ink, 1854)

57. JOHN EVERETT MILLAIS : STUDY FOR LORENZO AND ISABELLA (Pencil, 1848)

58. JOHN EVERETT MILLAIS : THE RACE-MEETING (Pen and ink, 1853)

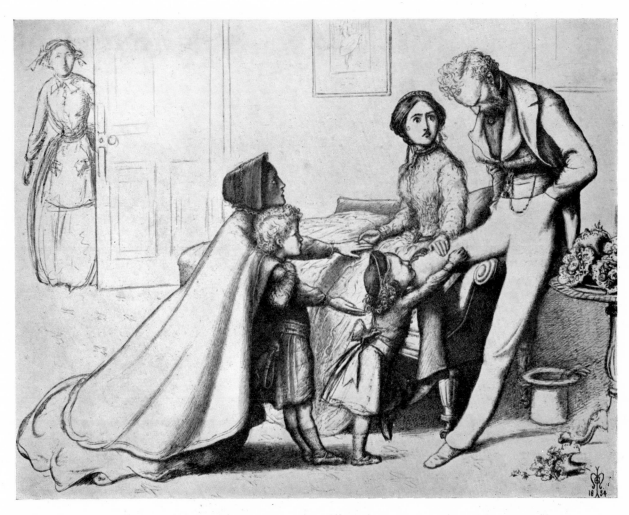

59. JOHN EVERETT MILLAIS : RETRIBUTION (Pen and ink, 1854)

Accepted

John Everett Millais
1853

60.   JOHN EVERETT MILLAIS : ACCEPTED (Pen and ink, 1853)

61. JOHN EVERETT MILLAIS : REJECTED (Pen and ink, 1853)

62.   JOHN EVERETT MILLAIS : FERDINAND AND ARIEL (Oil, 1849)

63. ARTHUR HUGHES : FERDINAND AND ARIEL (Oil)

64. ARTHUR HUGHES : FAIR ROSAMUND (Oil, 1854)

65. ARTHUR HUGHES : THE TRYST (Oil, c. 1854-55?)

66. ARTHUR HUGHES : HOME FROM WORK (Oil, 1861)

67. ARTHUR HUGHES : THE LONG ENGAGEMENT (Oil, 1853-59)

68. ARTHUR HUGHES : APRIL LOVE (Oil, 1856)

69. ARTHUR HUGHES : THE NATIVITY (Oil, 1858)

70. ARTHUR HUGHES : STUDY FOR "HOME FROM SEA" (Pen and ink, 1857)

71. HENRY WALLIS : THE DEATH OF CHATTERTON (Oil, 1856)

72. JOHN EVERETT MILLAIS : JOHN RUSKIN (Oil, 1853-54)

73. JOHN RUSKIN : GNEISS ROCK AT GLENFINLAS (Watercolour, 1853)

74. JOHN RUSKIN : THE *GLACIER DES BOISSONS* (Watercolour, 1849)

75. JOHN RUSKIN : COAST SCENE NEAR DUNBAR (Pen and watercolour, touched with bodycolour, 1857)

76. FREDERIC GEORGE STEPHENS : MOTHER AND CHILD (Oil, c. 1849)

77. JOHN BRETT : THE STONEBREAKER (Oil, 1857-58)

78. JOHN BRETT : FEBRUARY IN THE ISLE OF WIGHT (Watercolour and bodycolour, 1866)

79. JOHN BRETT : THE VAL D'AOSTA (Oil, 1858-59)

80. EDWARD BURNE-JONES : THE MAGIC CIRCLE (Watercolour, c. 1880?)

81. EDWARD BURNE-JONES : CLERK SANDERS (Watercolour, 1861)

82. EDWARD BURNE-JONES : KING COPHETUA AND THE BEGGAR-MAID (Oil, 1884)

83.   EDWARD BURNE-JONES : AURORA (Oil, 1896)

84. EDWARD BURNE-JONES : THE ARMING OF PERSEUS (Oil, c. 1875)

85.   EDWARD BURNE-JONES : THE CALL OF PERSEUS (Oil, c. 1875)

86.   EDWARD BURNE-JONES : STUDY OF ARMOUR (Bodycolour, c. 1875)

87. EDWARD BURNE-JONES : A ZITHERN PLAYER (Black, bronze and gold ink, 1896)

88. EDWARD BURNE-JONES : THE BRIAR ROSE: THE SLEEPING KNIGHTS IN THE BRIAR WOOD (Oil, c. 1870)

89. EDWARD BURNE-JONES : THE GARDEN OF PAN (Oil, 1886-87)

90. EDWARD BURNE-JONES : SHEET OF STUDIES FOR DECORATIONS AT THE RED HOUSE (Watercolour, 1860)

91.   EDWARD BURNE-JONES : GREEN SUMMER (Watercolour and bodycolour, 1864)

92.   WILLIAM MORRIS : LA BELLE ISEULT (Oil, 1858)

93. WILLIAM MORRIS : ST. GEORGE (Pen and ink, 1861)

94. FREDERIC LEIGHTON : A LEMON TREE (Pencil, 1859)

INDEX OF COLLECTIONS

MUSEUMS AND GALLERIES

PRIVATE COLLECTIONS IN GREAT BRITAIN